The **Best Tennis** of **Your Life**

50 Mental Strategies for Fearless Performance

Jeff Greenwald

Foreword by Jim Loehr, Ed.D.

BETTERWAY BOOKS
Cincinnati, Ohio

For more fine books from F+W Publications, visit our online bookstore at www.fwpublications.com.

Distributed in Canada by Fraser Direct, 100 Armstrong Avenue, Georgetown, ON, Canada L7G 5S4, Tel: (905) 877-4411. Distributed in the U.K. and Europe by David & Charles, Brunel House, Newton Abbot, Devon, TQ12 4PU, England, Tel: (+44) 1626 323200, Fax: (+44) 1626 323319, E-mail: postmaster@davidandcharles.co.uk. Distributed in Australia by Capricorn Link, P.O. Box 704, Windsor, NSW 2756 Australia, Tel: (02) 4577-3555.

20 19 18 17 16   15 14 13 12 11

Library of Congress Cataloging-in-Publication Data
Greenwald, Jeff.
  The best tennis of your life : 50 mental strategies for fearless performance / by Jeff Greenwald. -- 1st ed.
     p. cm.
  Includes index.
  ISBN 978-1-55870-844-0 (pbk. : alk. paper)
  1. Tennis--Training. I. Title.

  GV1002.9.T7G75 2008
  796.342071--dc22

                                                        2007034123

Edited by Michelle Ehrhard
Designed by Wendy Dunning
Production coordinated by Mark Griffin

Dedication

For my wife, Becca, and my parents, Howard and Marilynn Greenwald, for their loving support on and off the court.

Acknowledgments

I would like to acknowledge the following people who supported me in creating this book: my editor, Michelle Ehrhard, for her belief and support of this book from the very beginning; my agent, Bob Diforio, for his energy and focus in helping this book become a reality; and all of the players, coaches, and parents with whom I've worked over the years. It was your personal stories, triumphs, and struggles that inspired me to write this book.

About the Author

Jeff Greenwald, M.A., MFT is a nationally recognized sport psychology consultant, working with numerous players from around the world on their mental game. Prior to receiving his master's degree in clinical and sport psychology from John F. Kennedy University in 1997, Jeff coached numerous nationally ranked juniors in both the United States and Germany. He is also a consultant for the United States Tennis Association and conducts frequent workshops for high-performance coaches and players. Jeff is also a licensed marriage and family therapist.

As a player, Jeff was ranked number one in the world by the ITF in the men's 35 age division and number one in the United States in singles and doubles in 2001. In 1988, at the University of California at Santa Barbara, Jeff was named Athlete of the Year. He attended the Nick Bollettierri Academy and was nationally ranked throughout his junior career.

Jeff is the author of Amazon's best-selling double-CD audio program, *FearlessTennis: The 5 Mental Keys to Unlocking Your Potential*. He lives with his wife and daughter in San Rafael, California. Jeff can be reached via his Web site at www.mentaledge.net and e-mails can be sent to jeff@mentaledge.net.

Table of Contents

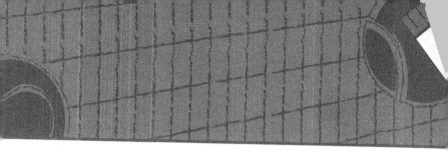

Foreword

I made the decision to pursue a career in sport psychology in 1976. I was Chief Psychologist and Executive Director of a large community mental health center that served the central and southern part of Colorado. When I announced my resignation to the center's twenty-three-member board of directors and explained that I wanted to pursue a career in sport psychology, it was as if I told them that I was moving to planet Mars to work. Dismay, confusion and disbelief was their response. In 1976, virtually no one had ever heard of sport psychology. I was leaving a fabulous job for a career that really didn't exist yet. How could I do such a foolish thing was the question on most everyone's mind.

Three decades later I'm still not completely sure what moved me to launch a completely new career path. I do know that the application of psychology to sport ignited passion and excitement in me that I'd never known before. I became intoxicated by the work and now feel so grateful for having had the opportunity to contribute to the developing field of performance psychology.

I think Jeff Greenwald comes from the same mold. I've known Jeff for many years and have seen first hand his devotion to the field, his attention to detail, his willingness to do whatever it takes to make a real contribution. I fully understand his passion and commitment. So much new ground has been covered by researchers, writers, and practitioners since 1976. Literally hundreds of books have been published world wide on the mental side of tennis but Jeff's book, *The Best Tennis of Your Life: 50 Mental Strategies for Fearless Performance* is in a very special class. I determine the value and contribution of new publications in the area of applied sport psychology by asking the following five questions: (1) is the book's content consistent with the latest and most responsible body of research in the field of sport psychology; (2) is the material written in a highly accessible, easy to understand language for athletes; (3) are the book's suggestions and recommendations practical and doable for most athletes; (4) does the book's content reflect an in-depth understanding of the complex dynamics and nuances of the sport it is intended for; (5) does the book offer new and original insights that are not available in previously written publications? Jeff's new book clearly meets all five benchmarks.

There are several things that I really like about this book. From the very first page, it is clear that this is not material written by an armchair psychologist. This is a book for players written by a real player. Jeff's competitive experience and his climb to number one in the world in the 35s brings depth, dimension and authenticity to his voice and to his suggestions. Tennis players seeking competitive help will not be disappointed by having to endure pages of abstract theory and research references. Although Jeff's work is based on sound theory and research, the book consistently delivers sound advice that can be translated into practice almost immediately.

Perhaps the most unique and valuable aspect of Jeff's book is the presentation format for his ideas and recommendations. Every one of the fifty chapters represents a short, highly specific learning segment for the reader. Tennis competitors can go right to what they need and get practical advice in an assessable, condensed form. Because of this, players will use this book as a valuable reference guide and repeatedly go back to it time and again in their quest to achieve mastery of the mental side of sport.

The real drama of sport is not the battle to see who has the deepest reservoir of talent and skill but rather who can summon whatever reservoir they have when it really matters—in the crucible of unrelenting pressure. Jeff's approach to fearless tennis represents a real contribution to the field of applied sport psychology and is a must read for every serious competitive tennis player. You will not be disappointed.

Jim Loehr, Ed.D.
Best-Selling Author
CEO & Chairman
Human Performance Institute

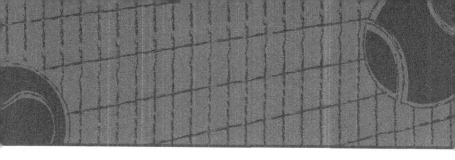

Introduction

For years, while in college and on the pro tour, I struggled with
the disappointment that I wasn't playing my best tennis, especially
when a match was close. In too many matches, I was a victim of
my nerves and was hesitant to really hit through my shots and risk
missing. Don't get me wrong, most of the time it was very subtle—a
backhand I wouldn't hit down the line when I had the opening or
an offensive return of serve on break point. Even when other people
told me I played well, deep down, I knew that I could play better if
only I could master the mental game.

I've always been deeply curious about why we make the choices we
do (especially when they aren't helpful), what motivates us to achieve
and excel, and how to make lasting changes that can truly impact our
lives. This curiosity peaked when I was playing club tennis in Ham-
burg, Germany. As I became more appreciative of my ability to play
the game of tennis, my whole approach to the game began to shift,
and I started to experience more joy on the court. Inspired to learn
more about how we can harness the power of the mind on the tennis

court, I decided to leave Germany and immerse myself into a clinical and sport psychology program. After I finished graduate school and spent some time with renowned sport psychologist, Jim Loehr, Ed.D., it was important to me to continue competing so I could test the concepts, skills, and strategies I was learning on my own. Even though I get excited about the change process and possibility of improvement, I am also a healthy skeptic. The evolution took some time. But match by match, with my willingness to experiment with the tools presented in this book, I found a mindset that catapulted me to the next level. As I became more aware of myself and how I needed to feel and think on the court, I was freed up to go for my shots. I enjoyed playing the game more than ever. I trusted my body to execute, and the balls started landing in. This led to more wins, and my confidence and self-image as a player grew. Ultimately, it ended in my earning the number one International Tennis Federation (ITF) world and U.S. rankings in my age group in 2001.

I have also been touched by the letters and e-mails I have received from players after the release of my audio program, *FearlessTennis*. Players of all levels have written telling me how, for the first time in their lives, they are playing more carefree and enjoying the game more than they have in a long time. I am grateful to all of you who have shared your personal challenges and stories with me over the years.

In addition to my own experience as a player and coach, this book, *The Best Tennis of Your Life*, grew out of hundreds of conversations with other players who, on varying levels, have struggled to play their best consistently. In particular, players confessed to me how difficult it has been to feel loose, focused, and confident on the court, especially in matches and under pressure. What has been most intriguing and frustrating to me is how the mental skills they have learned over the years have only sporadically translated to competition. I can empathize with this challenge. This book reflects my quest to shrink the gap between what you learn and what you actually do when it counts. Through fifty practical strategies and inspirational stories about clients with whom I've worked over the years, my own trials and tribulations as a competitor, and examples from the best in the game, it is my hope that you find the strategies you need to master the mental game.

Deep down, I believe that you know when you play with courage and without fear. You know when you play to win, maintain composure under pressure, and truly go for your shots. You also know when you don't and how frustrated you feel when you repeat old patterns or succumb to your nasty inner critic. To move out of your comfort zone, like I had to do, you need to be tired of the pain of knowing that you are selling out and have far more ability than you probably even realize. It is my hope that this book helps you break through your own personal barrier, that it inspires you to take more risks and play the game on your own terms. I want you to say that you are the kind of player who plays better when the pressure is on, that you've learned to love the game even more, and that you cherish the opportunities before you.

Tennis is a very forgiving game and can teach you a lot about yourself. Opportunities to improve, take risks, and challenge yourself will present themselves again and again.

Ultimately, it is up to you whether you choose to step out of what is familiar in the service of learning, improving, and personal triumph. Once you make the choice to practice the skills and strategies presented in this book and commit to using them, you will experience a freedom and level of performance you have witnessed on only a few occasions. I hope this book helps guide you even closer to playing the best tennis of your life.

1

Find Pleasure in Pressure

I've been asked how the best players in the world compete so well when the stakes are so high. "How do players deal with the stress with so much on the line?" Answer: They learn to thrive on it. Do you know what Pete Sampras told *Inside Tennis* after his retirement when asked what he missed the most about the game? He said, "I miss feeling so nervous that I would throw up before the finals of Wimbledon." Finding pleasure in pressure is a critical mind-set if you want to compete at higher and higher levels in the game.

Watching Andre Agassi and Marcos Baghdatis battle off match points in the fifth set of the 2006 U.S. Open and hit winners with their bodies pushed to the limit, it's hard not to be impressed. These players have certainly found a mind-set that works. Though consistent training, superior talent, and skill naturally all play an integral part in the ability to execute under pressure, embracing the feeling of pressure could certainly be useful as you try to improve your odds of winning that 5–4 game in the third set to grab a win. It all comes down to what pressure means and feels like to you. Do you really want to be there? Or are you secretly wishing you could be in the stands watching rather than playing? I suggest you identify your true mind-set.

Pressure is subjective. The amount of pressure you feel will depend on your belief in your ability to handle the situation at hand. For example, when you are in the third set, you need to trust your strokes and embrace the moment rather than think of either the past or future. Even when the butterflies are swarming in your stomach and your heart is racing, the difference between success and failure in that moment lies in how you perceive the situation. Are you scared or excited about the opportunity before you?

Your challenge is to see close matches as opportunities to challenge yourself, dig deep, and execute your shots regardless of how nervous you may feel. When you view your nerves as signals that indicate excitement and opportunity, you will play better. In his book, *Driven From Within*, Michael Jordan says, "The day I don't feel nervous is the day I know I must quit the game of basketball." Regardless of his nerves, Michael always wanted the ball. He viewed his nerves in a very positive light and always grabbed the opportunity to play and improve.

When you embrace pressure, you begin to enjoy it, even thrive on it. When you feel as though your back is against the wall, this is the time to reach deeply into your guts and stand tall. The team, fans, parents, or media may all be watching what you do next, but this fades into the background as you focus intently on your goal. The ability to embrace pressure like this will become your greatest memory one day as you reflect on your experience in the game.

To embrace and enjoy pressure, you first need to acknowledge and accept your physical tension. Don't try to cover it up by playing tentatively or rushing through your shots. This is critical. You need to understand that your tension is actually the catalyst to peak performance. You need it. Without it, your best tennis will not emerge. Do not be scared of it; use it. Breathe and smile to yourself as you decide to channel this energy into the ball. It simply means that you care and are excited to be in this moment.

Next time you go up 5–4 in the third serving, feel a pang of nervous energy, and find yourself hoping your opponent will hand you the match with some loose errors, remind yourself, "I love this. I wouldn't want to be anywhere else."

Play With Gratitude

One of the best ways to replicate your best day on the court is to remember to be grateful for the moment you are in right now.

We now have conclusive evidence from magnetic resonance imaging (MRI) scans of the brain and more dependable biofeedback procedures that a feeling of gratitude or deep appreciation can impact the entire nervous system, including how the brain functions. The connection between gratitude and the body has exciting implications, particularly as it relates to tennis performance.

Feelings of gratitude will almost always have a calming effect that will lower your tension level. Being grateful is acceptance in its purest form. It's difficult to be worrying about the future, to be wishing you had a better draw, or to be angry at yourself for losing the last point when you become aware of the bigger picture—you're alive, doing something you love with an opportunity to learn and improve. Being grateful requires you to expand your perspective. Next time you're at a tournament, take a step back and remind yourself how fortunate you are to be there. You are most likely relatively fit and healthy; otherwise you probably wouldn't be competing at all. Ask yourself if you would really want to be anywhere else at that moment. I hope the answer is no!

In *The Art of Happiness*, the Dalai Lama acknowledges the power we all possess to alter our state of mind. He explains:

> As time goes on, you can make positive changes. Every day as soon as you get up, you can develop a sincere positive motivation, thinking, "I will utilize this day in a more positive way. I should not waste this very day." Moving to a more grateful state of mind is a choice that can become a habit.

I, too, have trained myself to get into a more grateful state of mind before matches. As soon as my feet hit the floor in the morning, I feel myself walking and make a point to appreciate my body. I am thankful that I have a day ahead of me to run, hit, and compete. I reflect on how lucky I am to have this opportunity. This process puts me in a more present state of mind on the court so that everything I do leading up to the match is enjoyable and part of the whole process of competing. I realize that it is not only about winning, even though that is an important goal, too. For me, the match is a gift, and I walk on the court with this feeling inside me. It helps me focus and stay loose.

You can do the same. To help you get into a more grateful state, take a few minutes before your match, or on the morning of your match, to close your eyes, and breathe while you reflect on what you like so much about tennis; embrace the feeling you have. Recognize that today is another day to improve and enjoy doing something you love. We're not taking any of our wins or losses with us, so do your best to enjoy the moment and embrace the challenge before you. This is a mind-set that can be strengthened and one that is available to you if you choose to access it. By doing so, you will begin to start matches with more calmness and confidence, you will become less upset when you make errors, and you will maintain your focus, particularly when a match is close. A sense of gratitude on changeovers and in difficult situations will help you develop the perspective you need to execute your shots with authority. You will become extremely tough to beat, and, most importantly, you will get more joy out of hitting the ball than ever before.

3

Separate Productive Worry From Unproductive Worry

Worry gets the best of us all at one time or another. It destroys performance and causes us to play tentatively and doubt ourselves. It makes competition stressful and frustrating, affecting our enjoyment of the game. To end this experience, we need to understand the difference between productive worry and unproductive worry.

First, it's important to acknowledge that some worry can actually be productive, propelling you to string your racquets ahead of time, pack your bag with the essentials before the match, decide on your game plan, and make sure you have a court and partner to warm up with—all of which is time well spent. Similarly, if you find yourself worrying about your technique in the weeks leading up to your tournament because a stroke feels a bit off, this may propel you to spend more time honing your game. The reason these are all considered productive worries is because you can do something about them; in other words, they are *within your control*.

However, if you are worrying about things that are *outside your control*, this would be considered unproductive worry. For example, worrying about whether you will win or lose, what other people might think of you if you lose, and how your ranking might drop would all fall into the unproductive bucket. In fact, these types of thoughts generate feelings of anxiety, which will generally make you play worse. Without taking control of your worry, you will certainly lose confidence and be distracted from the thoughts and actions that help you play better. Edward Hallowell, author of the best-selling book *Driven to Distraction*, describes it this way:

> The human imagination, at times the great tool of creation, is at other times our bane, as it snoops into the crevices of life to find, or even to create, phantoms of devils of every species and style, ready to tease and torment us as we attempt to pass the day in peace.

My test came in September 2001, the night before I was to play the finals of the Men's 35 ITF World Championships in Portschau, Austria. I was in my hotel room and found myself worrying about the upcoming match. I knew that if I won the next day, I would earn the year-end ranking of number one in the world and number one in the United States that year in my age group. As my thoughts raced about the impact of this match, I became nervous about the prospect of losing, wondering, *Will I play well? What if I don't win?* After stewing about the meaning of the match, I finally grabbed ahold of myself and said, *Jeff, you have no control over whether you win or lose tomorrow. Just focus on getting prepared—hydrate, stretch, and visualize playing well.* It worked. I changed the channel in my head. I switched my focus and stopped worrying about what I couldn't control and made a choice to focus on my game plan and preparing myself. I ended up winning the ITF World Championships the next day.

Even when your mind starts to get away from you, you have the choice to shift your mind-set once you become aware of your thoughts.

Next time you find yourself worrying about an upcoming tournament, your game, or what might happen to your ranking, ask yourself: *Can I do anything about this right now?* If the answer is no, detach yourself from the thought and drop the worry. If the answer is yes, find time to make a list of things you can do, step-by-step, to productively work toward your goals. The key is to learn to let go of the unproductive worry (out of your control) and get back to actions that will help you achieve your goals.

I trust that you, too, can fend off the worry that comes knocking on your door once you recognize which type of worry you are engaging in.

4

Use Winning and Losing as Springboards for Future Success

When I was a younger, winning and losing were my only measures of progress. It was this outcome focus that prevented me from playing freely for years. I remember well the feeling of fear and regret when I missed a backhand long at the "wrong" time. Of course, looking through my narrow lens at the time, it was always the "wrong" time. In my mind, mistakes or a loss meant that I simply wasn't measuring up and I was blowing my opportunities. It turned out that this mind-set, more than the actual error or negative result, was my greatest obstacle. It was a restrictive mind-set caught in what wasn't working, rather than on what I could learn or do differently. Over the years, with some self-reflection, I began to recognize that errors—and even losing—were not only part of the game but provided information that would ultimately help me develop my game further and win more.

The key to turning the pain of missing and losing into something positive is learning to use the results as information about you and your game. In other words, when you think that your mistakes mean you don't have the ability you thought you had, you will begin to doubt yourself—a mind-set you can't afford to have in this game. Rather, you need to view your less-than-satisfactory performances as temporary blips that are within your control. By doing so, you will remain calmer, give yourself a chance to dig down, and come up with the win, even when your game feels off.

Roger Federer is a great example of a player who has learned to maintain his composure even when things aren't going his way. However, he wasn't always like this. His parents removed his privilege of playing tennis when he was younger, because of his angry outbursts, which gave him more respect for the importance of staying composed on the court.

Of course, there is a natural level of disappointment in a lost opportunity when you lose, but you need to view this as only a minor bump in the road. The more accomplished pro players seem to view winning and losing in a more "businesslike" fashion. At the 2003 U.S. Open, for example, I ran into Scott Draper, who reached a career high of number forty-two in the world, and I asked him about his recent match against Roger Federer just two weeks after Federer won his second Wimbledon. With six match points to win the match against Federer, Scott, rather nonchalantly, reported in his Australian accent, "Yeah, I did all that I could. I hit the right shots, played him smart, but he came up with some unbelievable stuff. There was nothing to feel bad about." Scott's matter-of-fact perspective appears to be reflective of his need to learn, move on, and accept the hard reality of competing at this level for one's livelihood. This process-based mind-set is critical at this level of the game, given the pressure and need to constantly learn and improve. It's not a surprise that he became one of the first players ever to win a professional golf tournament after his retirement from the game of tennis.

Let mistakes propel you back to the practice court as quickly as possible. Try to be clear about what skills need work and don't allow your mind to cast doubt on your long-term ability. Don't be afraid to acknowledge the truth about your weaknesses. Instead of being frustrated about your mistakes, try to use them as springboards for future success. You need to believe that you can improve and win again. "I was pretty mad after the U.S. Open," Andy Roddick recently said in *Inside Tennis* after securing a win in the recent Davis Cup match. "I was pretty hungry here. I felt like I needed to prove myself all over again."

Avoid the trap of thinking too short-term. All success and mastery are built on numerous mistakes and losses. Set specific long-term goals and work toward these with passion, always using your losses and mistakes as information and learning opportunities.

5

Behave Your Way Into the Zone

Sometimes the best way to get yourself into the zone is by acting your way there.

If you watched Roger Federer and Rafael Nadal in the 2006 Wimbledon finals, you may have noticed how the game's best have learned to create the right mix of emotions in competition. You saw Federer's relaxed stride as he strutted onto the court to defend his title for the fifth time, while his nemesis, Rafael Nadal, sprinted back to the baseline after the coin toss like a kid on Christmas morning. One also can't help but notice Maria Sharapova's incessant fist pumping that has become almost as predictable as her grunt. One thing you can be sure of is that these world-class athletes know exactly what they are doing—they are behaving their way into the zone.

Their behavior makes good sense. For years we have known that the human mind is wired to make associations. When our physical actions are connected to positive emotional experiences, these actions become powerful triggers in the future. If Nadal's trademark sprint becomes a routine—either before a match, following a moment of clutch play, or during a momentum swing—that same move will eventually become a helpful trigger at a time when he may need an emotional tune-up. The same holds true for you. When you behave in a positive manner, often the emotions and mind-set follow.

Federer's relaxed and confident walk certainly helps him maintain the looseness that is characteristic of his entire game. Nadal's sprint to the baseline has the effect of raising his heart rate, increasing his intensity so that he can embrace and harness his nervous energy. Sharapova's fist pump is a reminder to fight and to recapture or maintain her sense of momentum.

Both Jim Loehr, in his book *Mental Toughness Training for Sports: Achieving Athletic Excellence,* and Mihaly Csikszentmihalyi, author of *Flow in Sports*, have been enormously helpful in identifying the key factors related to a player's ideal performance state and the concept of "flow." The important next step is for players to cultivate and access this state effectively when under pressure or feeling tight.

Unquestionably, all competitive players know how challenging it can be to consistently create the right mix of emotions week in and week out. However, this experience does not need to be reserved for the likes of Federer, Nadal, and Sharapova. You, too, can train yourself to get closer to this mind-body state.

For example, notice your ideal walking pace—that is, when you are in a good mental place and feeling confident on or off the court. What is your walking pace and body posture like when you feel positive and upbeat? See if the pace of your walk in this state can be applied to your between-point walk on the court. See if it helps you generate a rhythm that feels more energizing and confident.

Experiment with your walking posture (for example, walking tall with your shoulders back) and see if you feel more confident and in control. The moves may be subtle, but the emotional impact can often be dramatic.

Personally, as I am now more aware of my physical presence in competition, I notice that when I am playing well, the pace of my walk between points is slightly quicker—a pace that reflects confidence and intention. Between points, I walk with my shoulders back, with my eyes on the ground or on my strings, to help me maintain my focus. Another nuance I notice when I am successful is that when I miss a shot and lose the point, I often smile, as if to say, *I know. But I'm still in charge here.*

You don't have to be a Federer, Nadal, or Sharapova to behave your way into the zone. Develop your body awareness so that you can act how you want to feel, with a renewed determination to commit to your shots, regardless of the circumstance. Then watch as you begin to move closer to repeating your best day more often.

6

Momentum Is With You
If You Think It Is

I used to feel a sense of dread when I would miss a volley with a wide-open court. In that instant, I felt the momentum turn against me. I have since learned that momentum shifts are often within our control. It is a subjective experience and can be influenced by the way we think about a particular moment. If you think the momentum is with you or against you, you are probably right. Therefore, you need to be mindful of how you interpret the situation.

If you happened to see the James Blake/Andre Agassi U.S. Open quarterfinal match in 2005, you understand how momentum can shift on a dime. Agassi, down two sets to love, with Blake serving for the match, appeared to redirect the momentum swing before fans' eyes by hitting a couple of inside-out forehands that clipped the lines. Clearly, Agassi didn't view the momentum the way most of the fans, or possibly Blake himself, did. Rather, he hunkered down, played fearlessly, won a few key points, and literally stole the momentum back and went on to the final.

But what is momentum? And, more importantly, how can you use it to your advantage? While research conclusions are still mixed on what actually causes momentum shifts to occur, it is now clear that psychological momentum does exist. Therefore, gaining more awareness of the factors that seem to generate feelings of momentum can be very useful. Can you recall the feeling? Do you recall having a sense of control, more motivation, increased self-confidence, concentration, and even a slight rise in your energy level?

Typically, when we think of momentum, we think of a situation in which a player wins a string of points or games or produces a clutch shot when the score is close. However, the truth is that momentum swings like this are much more complex and, most importantly, involve your personal interpretation of the situation. For example, if you believe that you are still in control and that momentum has *not* shifted (you believe you can come back, and you have a plan in mind), then it has *not* shifted. Similarly, if your opponent doubts that he or she can keep the winning going (many players do begin to worry about this), then momentum is technically up for grabs. I can't tell you how many matches I've won and seen others win after being down 5–2 or 5–1 in the third. Just win a game or two, and the other player's perception of momentum can often shift as well.

Most of the time, you determine whether momentum has shifted or not. Your thoughts and responses in the situation will play a crucial role in determining what happens in the subsequent games. Alistair Higham, Lawn Tennis Association (LTA) head coach of relations in the United Kingdom and author of *Momentum: The Hidden Force in Tennis*, described it to me this way, "Understanding the power of momentum and maintaining a positive perspective through the ebbs and flows of a match can greatly impact its outcome."

Next time you find yourself behind in competition, remind yourself that momentum is with you if you think it is. Remember that your opponent may doubt whether she can actually finish what she's started. If you're the one with the momentum, remember that you are still in control of your thoughts, feelings, and behavior—all of which can impact whether momentum is working for you or against you.

7

Focus Your Attention on What Matters

As our attention spans shrink and distractions increase with the addition of the Internet and cell phones, focusing your mind in the present is a formidable challenge. But, certainly when it comes to tapping into your best tennis, this skill is paramount.

When I conduct workshops on the mental game, the issue of focus is one of the most common challenges players present to me. How do you *not* think about the score? How can you keep your mind on each point rather than focus on all the other distractions around you?

I believe the reason that focus is one of the most widely acknowledged yet underdeveloped skills among players of all levels is that it is not practiced enough—on or off the court. Like any technical skill we develop, a focused mind also requires training. To wipe away the distracting thoughts, particularly when a situation feels "big" to you, is perhaps the single most difficult yet critical skill you can learn. To execute your shots without interference from your mind is a worthy goal and one that is achievable. "A calmness develops with intensive concentration practice that has a remarkably stable quality to it," says

Jon Kabat-Zinn, a leader in the field of mindfulness and meditation and author of *Wherever You Go, There You Are: Mindfulness Meditation in Everyday Life*. "It is steadfast, profound, hard to disturb, no matter what comes up. It is a great gift to oneself."

Being focused in the present is a mind-body experience in which our attention is directed to what is "relevant" in the moment. We are not at the office, at home making dinner, going through our daily to-do lists, or worrying about our ranking, self-image, or approval from coaches or parents. This clutter is gone. This clutter is removed when we make a conscious choice to engage in the present moment.

Do you remember Pete Sampras's second serve ace against Àlex Corretja in the quarterfinals of the U.S. Open in 1996 when he was down match point? Sampras, like many world-class players, learned to maintain a pinpoint focus on the task at hand—something we all forget to do, especially when a match is close. In this moment, Sampras was not thinking about the paycheck, whether people in the stands approved of him, or that if he pulled this out he would have another Grand Slam under his belt. Rather, when he approached the line to serve, after having practically dropped to the ground, he focused his attention on the spot where he was going to serve, and that's it. No second-guessing and no worrying about his self-image, choking, his ranking, the benefit of winning this match, or whom he was playing. He pictured where he was going to hit the ball and then performed.

This is your challenge as well: to focus your attention on what you control in the moment—your attitude, where you want to hit the ball, and staying loose.

To train your mind to be present, pay more attention to physical sensations throughout the day while you play or work. Be more aware of your body in a nonjudgmental way. This process will deepen your feeling of presence in the moment. For example, feel the chair you are sitting in right now, notice your breath, pay attention to your feet on the ground while walking, etc. Also, practice keeping your attention on things longer than you normally do. Before matches, track things longer with your eyes. Avoid rushing and try not to let your eyes dart around very much. You will be surprised how helpful it can be to consciously pay attention to objects around you. As anxiety increases, the eyes begin to lose focus. Keeping your eyes focused will help you become more present and decrease your anxiety while your attention deepens. When you are on the court, keep your eyes focused on the ground, your strings, the ball, and specific targets where you are hitting. Feel the racquet and balls in your hand. All these actions will increase the likelihood that you stay in the present moment.

I know that you, too, can experience the power of a focused mind in the present—focusing on what is relevant and not on the outcome. This ability to be present will help you enjoy the game more, feel more in control of your mind, and make playing the game feel effortless.

8

Loosen Up When It Counts

Given the pressure to win, expectations we create in our minds, and self-doubt that we all experience from time to time, it is not surprising that staying "loose" in competition continues to be our greatest challenge. I use the word *loose* because playing relaxed is not only unrealistic, it is counterproductive. This is because you actually need a certain amount of arousal or adrenaline to play your best. Rather, the goal is to learn how to drop into a looser physical state even when adrenaline is surging through your body. When you learn how to access this state and can release tension more effectively, you will be a whole lot looser to execute your shots with confidence.

Unfortunately, in 1988 when I was a senior at the University of California Santa Barbara, I didn't have this tool. I remember that I was playing the number-one player from the University of California Los Angeles in his stadium court—he was also ranked number one in the United States at the time. If I won the match, I would likely go to the National Collegiate Athletic Association's (NCAA) competition, given my record that year. I was playing aggressively and remember taking the lead 6–4, 4–1. All of a sudden, while I was waiting to return serve, I was hit by the thought, *If I win this match, I'm going to the NCAAs.* Within seconds, a surge of adrenaline rushed through my body, and my arm tightened up. I remember being self-conscious about the rush of nerves, and I began playing tentatively and backing off the ball. I told myself to relax, but it didn't help. It actually made it worse. I became fearful of missing. The high level of tennis I was accessing a moment before disappeared in an instant. I became a *victim* of my nerves. And, to no surprise, I ended up losing the match—a painful blow, I must admit.

In my experience, getting the body loose when the nervous system is ramping up is a worthy pursuit, and achievable. The benefits are numerous: self-confidence, greater enjoyment, more passion, and, ultimately, results. However, most players don't have a reliable way to maintain this ideal level of looseness when their nerves or negative thoughts kick in.

Once you become better at "dropping" into a looser physical state, the nerves will no longer be so destructive to your performance. What happens is that many players recognize that they are overly tight, and their brains immediately tell them, *This is not good. You have to relax.* Of course, as most of us know, this command-and-control style simply doesn't work. As Patrick Rafter told *Inside Tennis* after he lost in the semifinals of Wimbledon years ago, "I told myself to relax, and I got tighter. Next year, I think I'll tell myself to get tight and see what happens." Getting into a looser state, however, doesn't need to be such a mystery.

Even the best players struggle with physical tension from time to time. The key is to become aware of your body so that you can literally "call up" the feeling of looseness when your body tightens up. One way to do this is to shift your attention into your arms and shoulders (called a "body scan") and check for any excess tension before you serve or return. The simple act of acknowledging the tension, accepting it, and releasing it with a deep breath can make a huge difference when executing your shots. In Mihaly Csikszentmihalyi's book *Finding Flow: The Psychology of Engagement With Everyday Life*, he remarks how being tuned into the body in this way can help greatly. "The more attention we invest in the body and its performance, the less is left over to ruminate about saving face or impressing others. In a paradoxical way, it is often by paying attention to your body that you get to forget the ego." Remembering to tune into your body on the court and checking your tension levels from time to time, acknowledging the tension, and then breathing it out by saying, "Let go," can be enormously helpful. Getting out of your head like this and into your body will make a huge difference.

Remember, getting loose when you are tense is an act of acceptance and awareness rather than self-consciousness and desire to "get rid" of the tension. Using the other relaxation techniques in chapters forty-two and forty-three will also help you train this feeling. If you don't train yourself to become more familiar with what loose feels like off the court, it will be very difficult to re-create that loose state when you need it.

By training this on and off the court, you will be better able to literally "hop" into a looser physical state, even in pressure situations. Of course, once you release the tension, you must commit to your shots and swing through the ball. This commitment is critical and will further loosen you up as you train your mind and body to do what they already know how to do.

9

Focus on Your Game, Not Your Opponent's Ranking

You're standing in front of the draw at the tournament. You can't help yourself as you scan your section of the draw. You see that you could play the fourth seed in the round of sixteen—if you make it there—and he's ranked significantly higher than you. But first you have to play an opponent ranked at least fifteen spots below you—a player you've played before, and you know won't go down easily. Your heart starts beating a little faster as your mind hops on the mental roller coaster and begins to evaluate your chances in the tournament. Stop. This is not the best mind-set to play your best tennis.

Players talking about how they "should" or "shouldn't" beat another player has become almost an epidemic in the world of competitive tennis. For a smoother and more successful ride in this game, I suggest that you remove *should* from your pre-match conversation and focus on your game, not on your opponent's ranking.

In a recent session debriefing a tournament match, a client told me, "I was nervous. I knew I *should* beat him. When I started to miss a few shots, I got angry and could never get it back." Sometime later in the conversation, my client then acknowledged, "I have always done well at nationals when I don't know the player at all."

I'm sure you can relate to this player's case of the "shoulds." Given the fact that he was ranked higher than his first opponent, his automatic thought, *I know I should beat him*, only hurt him (he ended up losing this match), as is most often the case. The problem is that with this "should" comes expectation, fear, loss of focus, and overconfidence.

You need to recognize that rankings are irrelevant during a tournament. They do not take into account how well you will play on a particular day, the surface you will be playing on, or your opponent's own mind-set. Rather, you need to go out with good intensity, go for your shots, and use your strengths. Of course, your mind wants to predict your chances of winning. Mentally tough players know they have control only over their emotional state. Before you get too swept away by all the predictions of your chances of winning or losing, try to remind yourself of your strengths—like your ability to outlast opponents, big serve and forehand, ability to take offense quickly, skill in moving the ball around, and quickness in coming to the net. Refocus attention on what you do well and strategize how you will use your strengths against your opponent's weaknesses. With this mind-set, you will be much better positioned to play well and win.

Begin catching yourself making assumptions based on who you are playing. Quickly, turn this thought around by saying, *It doesn't matter who I'm playing. I'm going to play my game and focus on one point at a time.* This will reroute your mind away from the expectation and pressure that you are creating to a more productive mind-set. Learning to embrace each match opportunity and focusing on your strengths, regardless of who you are playing, will bring you the most success.

10

Build Your Game
With a Vision

Change can be difficult. And, usually, it happens only when we are truly ready.

Everything written on the game of tennis related to strokes, strategy, mental toughness, or physical fitness asks us to consider changing our current habits if we want to improve our performance on any level. Whether it's returning serve with more authority, remaining composed after mistakes, engaging in a strength training program, or developing a weapon, the decision to change takes two things—motivation and confidence. In other words, for any real change to take place in your game or your life, you need to believe that such a change is important and that you have the confidence to attempt the change.

When Pete Sampras was sixteen years old, he and his coach, Pete Fischer, made the decision to change Sampras from a two-handed to a one-handed backhand. At the time, Sampras was ranked nationally in the boy's 16, and such a change at this late stage was considered very bold. But he did it. We'd probably all agree that, given Sampras's game style and personality, not to mention his fourteen Grand

Slam titles, the decision was a positive one. But what helped Sampras make this decision? First, Fischer communicated his own belief that Sampras had the ability to make this change, which Sampras seemed to accept. Second, and most importantly, Sampras felt it was important for his career in the long run and that he had the confidence to stick with it, even if he lost some matches along the way.

The trick is to get clear about your intention related to the specific change you want to make. Make it important. Connect it to a value you hold, beyond winning or losing. It must reflect your desire to improve, to test yourself, and to learn on some level. Then maintaining the confidence to persevere is critical. This will most likely require a perspective shift related to "success" and "failure" in the short-term. Whatever change you choose to make, you need to assess the level of importance and confidence you have prior to taking it on. Perhaps this will make the difference for you as you consider your next bold move on or off the court.

To do this, choose a behavior or part of your game you would like to change over the next month. On a scale of 1 to 10, rate how important this change is to you. Similarly, rate how confident you are that you can successfully make this change. If it is below a 6 in either category, ask and answer, *How would I close the gap between where I am now and where I would like to be?* Try to come up with at least three action items you could do to move toward your goal.

Next, ask yourself, *What perspective shift do I need to make?* To do this, you will want to connect this change to a value you hold (for example, actualizing potential, enjoyment, personal challenge, etc.) and write down why you are making this change. Decide why it is important to you. Having a purpose for your change will help you maintain the motivation needed to see it through.

11

Engage in the Learning Process

With our desire for immediate results and a lack of self-awareness, we often don't even see the learning opportunities in front of our eyes. Engaging in the learning process is a critical step toward achieving goals on the tennis court.

Recently, I was practicing my serve for an upcoming tournament. On the court next to me was a woman in her forties also hitting buckets of serves. However, what particularly stuck out was how she was responding to each serve. I quickly became intrigued. I noticed that when she missed her serve—even just by an inch or two—she would hang her head and then shake it from side to side, defeated. It truly looked like a nightmare for her. After watching her, I took special note of what I was thinking and doing when I missed my serve. I noticed that after each serve that went into the net, I would immediately assess the tension in my arm to make sure it was loose enough and then refocus my attention on my target or adjust my toss.

Interested in the disparity of our experiences, I walked up to the woman and asked, "What part of your serve are you working on?"

She quickly retorted, "I just wanted to get the ball in once before I leave. Is that too much to ask?" She then walked away in frustration with her head down.

What struck me on an even deeper level was the degree to which this woman was literally sabotaging the very thing she wanted so badly. She wanted to serve well, get the ball in the court, and feel good about her serve. Yet she was doing nothing to actually make this happen. While I was on the next court making adjustments and tuning in to how my body was feeling on the serve, she was spiraling around in the world of expectations, disappointment, and frustration, essentially "living in the problem." But don't misunderstand me. Her difficulty wasn't due to a lack of effort; her mind was stuck on the immediate result and seemed to forget the importance of focusing on the key things that would actually help her find a better rhythm.

It's really easy to hand over the keys to your own development and lose the opportunity to increase your self-awareness and confidence. Becoming aware of yourself and your approach to the game is critical if you are going to translate the skills you learn into competition. When a coach tells you to keep your shoulders turned, check this out in your own body. See if you can feel what you are being told. Be a participant in your own learning process. Remember, you are the only one in your body. Your experience and perceptions about what you are being told or what you feel play a big role in how quickly you will improve.

Learning how you learn is critical in this day and age with so much information and such a demand for instant results and success. We need to learn how to make adjustments in the moment when things aren't going our way. We need to become more tuned in to what we feel physically when we do things well. What technical changes feel right? What are we focused on when we are successful? We are responsible for our own learning. Nobody can do this for us.

Of course, approaching your game in this way requires a paradigm shift that views learning and improvement as a high priority. When you spend more time focusing on what you need to learn, you will find the results beginning to happen, perhaps with less effort than before.

To improve the rate at which you improve, you need to become more aware of how your body feels when it hits the ball well. Learn to tune in to your body. Keep your emotions out of it as best you can. Having more kinesthetic awareness (physical feeling—the tension in your body, your body positioning, feel of the ball at contact) will help you become more aware of what you may need to adjust in the middle of a match. The answer to improving lies more in your body than in your head. Try to stay out of your head and try to avoid analyzing. Let your body teach you, and then give this feedback to your coach. You have more knowledge in your body than you realize.

Visualize After Errors
and Before Matches

I am a very competitive player. I love winning and always have. Even at fifteen years old, I was determined to find a way to win more. So I learned to visualize.

What did I do? I made an appointment with a hypnotist (sport psychology was not on the map yet). In the hour that I spent with the hypnotist, I was instructed to relax, let go of my thoughts, and simply focus on his voice. Once he had me in a relaxed state, he began making suggestions about what a winning performance looked like. He had me choose a specific match and recall what I looked like when I was playing my best. I can still remember the spring in my step as I left his office that day. I felt like a lion that was let out of a cage.

It worked. The next day I went to play a sectional tournament and beat two players ranked ahead of me. I would be hard-pressed to find a match in the twenty-five years since that time where I didn't use visualization as a way to boost my confidence or manage errors.

In one study, roughly 96 percent of all Olympic athletes said they used visualization as a way to prepare for the Olympic Games. Many players have learned to do this naturally as they prepare their mind and body for competition.

To practice using this skill, you need to first relax your mind and body with deep abdominal breaths for about five minutes. (You can also refer to chapter forty-two on quieting your mind.) Ideally, find a quiet place to focus on your breathing. Once your mind is calm, begin imagining yourself hitting your favorite shots. Try to assimilate yourself into the picture—actually be yourself hitting the ball. If this feels too difficult, it is also effective to view yourself from an external perspective—as if you are watching yourself on video. The key here is to feel and see the ball off your racquet going toward your intended target. Imagining how your body feels when it hits the ball will help the picture become more real for you. If you can hear the sound of the ball, this will make the scene even more realistic for you. Take your time. Enjoy the images. Don't rush and don't worry if the images are blurry at first. Play out a few points in your head if you like. Once you've got some images, add in any elements you like that address your specific goals. Do you want to be more confident? More focused? Go ahead and see yourself playing confidently. See yourself walking tall and confidently between points. Feel what it's like to be confident and dictate play. Similarly, if you want to improve your focus, see yourself with blinders on. Imagine yourself not being flustered by anything. Once you've pictured some details related to your attitude and physical presence on the court, you may want to top the scene off by shaking hands with your opponent and walking off with the balls as the winner. The images and specific scenes you choose are up to you.

If you like this technique, you can use it the night before competition and up to one hour before your match. Most importantly, it should feel natural and not rushed.

Visualization is also helpful to fix minor technical flaws in matches. Rather than berating yourself and overanalyzing your errors, visualize yourself hitting the shot correctly.

Remember the old phrase, "A picture speaks a thousand words"? This wisdom is often underutilized when it comes to correcting technical errors in matches. It can be helpful to briefly picture yourself correctly hitting the shot you just missed. By doing this, you are more likely to stay positive and not overthink your strokes. For example, when I'm serving, I will occasionally picture the ball going directly toward my target. I do this very quickly and automatically. You can do the same with any shot. For example, if you want to clean up your return of serve, pull up a clear image of yourself returning the ball with confidence. I have an image of myself taking a short backswing with my weight moving toward the ball. It takes about two seconds to do this. This image sets my intention for the next shot without having to use my thinking mind. Pictures are simply more powerful than words and instructions.

It's also helpful to exaggerate your image because often what you think may be too much will probably end up being just right. The key is then to execute the shot you just visualized in your head. Have this image ready to go when you need it. Do this in your mind right now. What do you look like when you are hitting your return with confidence? What does your body look like when you hit the ball? Think about the most important thing you can do on your return (you can go through the same process with any shot you like). Hold these images clearly in your mind and refresh them from time to time so they stay current. The best way to keep them fresh is by using them in matches when you need them.

What you'll find when you visualize the correct swing in your mind is that you keep your mind less cluttered with thoughts. This helps you play as instinctively and automatically as possible. When you are playing your best, typically your mind is calm and thoughts are kept to a minimum.

Once you have your personal snapshots in your head, you will be able to successfully tune up your shots with minimal effort. Rather than going down the "command and control" road of fixing your mistakes, keep your mind calm and tuned in to restive images as you ease yourself back into the groove.

13

Don't Get Too Satisfied After a Big Win

At the 2005 U.S. Open, Giles Muller, ranked number sixty-eight in the world, swept by Andy Roddick, the world's number-three player. As is so often the case after a big win, Muller's brief run was stopped dead in its tracks in the very next round. Certainly, it brings to mind the question: How can players keep their winning momentum going, especially after significant wins?

The first obvious trap players face as they move through a tournament is getting overly focused on their tournament results. Once this mind-set kicks in, all kinds of thoughts tend to emerge: *Now I can't afford to lose. I beat a seed. What if I can't produce the same result tomorrow? My parents/coach/spouse would be so happy if I could win my next match, too.*

On the flip side, players may also find themselves getting too satisfied after a good win and lose their intensity for their next match. Often, they celebrate too soon. This attitude is subtle but still deadly. Players aren't the only ones affected by the euphoria that emerges through winning. Parents, teammates, and coaches can also get sucked in to the "result trap" and get excited too soon. And players pick up on this intensity. Though it is certainly gratifying for players to see the effect their result can have on people around them, it can also distract them from focusing on what will help them win the next day.

How do the best players in the world keep the winning going? The game's best have learned to maintain a keen focus after winning by paying attention to aspects of the game within their control—their prematch preparation, postmatch recovery period, and well-thought-out strategic plan for their next opponent. While there is always an inner satisfaction and sense of accomplishment after a win, top players understand the importance of staying on an even keel in order to repeat or build up on their last successful performance. Rather than celebrating too soon or placing unnecessary expectations on themselves, they discuss their strategy and debrief what they did well and what they need to do to improve for the next match. In addition, after a win, top players may have a coach or parent scout their next opponent while they stay out of the sun, hydrate, get a massage, and make sure their equipment is ready for the next day. Simply put, all the pieces that contribute to a winning performance are immediately set in motion. These players quietly cherish their win but don't have the same need to walk around the tournament to see how many people they've impressed.

Next time you pull out a win against a worthy opponent, allow yourself some time to relish the win and experience; then move on. Don't let the semifinals or finals be enough for you. Keep testing yourself until the tournament is over. Then write down what you learned and get back to the practice court!

14

Be Patient Against Pushers

At one time or another, we all find ourselves losing to a "pusher"—someone who just hits the ball back and doesn't play aggressively but rather waits for you to make a mistake. You know your strokes are better; you beat players they lose to. Not to worry, you're in good company. Most of us have struggled defeating this kind of player. If this happens to you, there is still hope, but more than likely you'll need to exercise more patience if you want to finally prevail over the slow-hitting, human backboard while you get out of your own way.

When playing pushers, be mindful of your tendency to become overly impatient or conservative. Given that they can't hurt you with any weapons, you don't need to rush your shots. Also, if you have lost to this type of player in the past, it is easy to get overly emotional. Make sure you aren't going for too much at inappropriate times or protecting against errors. Even with a prematch game plan, it is too easy to get frustrated at the slightest sign that the match is headed in the wrong direction—again. Naturally, since your ultimate goal is to get the upper hand on this particular player and win the match, your mind will be very susceptible to the scoreboard. Avoid the tendency to give up too soon or think too black and white just because of past results. One player said to me, "I always lose to pushers. I can't beat these kinds of players."

Slow things down and decide that you are there to go the distance, regardless of how long it takes. As Roger Federer told the reporter on the way out to his second-round match at the 2006 U.S. Open against Tim Henman (an old nemesis who had beaten Roger a total of six times in past meetings), when asked if he would like to have the match be done in three sets, "I have my extra shirts packed, so if it goes all five sets, that will be great, too." Beating players we have lost to but whom we feel we can beat takes patience and a willingness to work the point and not force opportunities prematurely.

Of course, this mentality becomes even more challenging against players who don't give you much pace, because you have more time to think and hesitate. Remember, these types of players want to suck you into playing their game or have you explode and go for too much since they don't have the weapons to hurt you.

Before the match, commit to your game plan. Have the mind-set that you will work the point and capitalize on opportunities when they present themselves. Avoid forcing your shots. This approach will translate into more composure and less muscle tension, allowing you to execute the shots you need. Pretty soon, you will view pushers as just another challenge you can overcome.

15

Strike the Balance Between Process and Outcome

Many players get stuck in a mind-set that is extremely outcome focused. While we can't deny the importance of results in the game—this is one of the main ingredients that make the game so fun and appealing—getting out of balance and forgetting the importance of the process is a very slippery slope. For ultimate success and satisfaction in the game, seek to strike the balance between the excitement of developing and playing the game and your results.

As I discuss in my audio CD program *FearlessTennis: The 5 Mental Keys to Unlocking Your Potential*, one can't forget how, years ago, after winning the U.S., Australian, and French opens, Mats Wilander admitted, "My entire career I dreamed of being number one. But when I finally achieved it and the initial excitement wore off, I felt nothing. I had no sense of elation or pride. I was the world champion, but so what? It got to the stage where I got more satisfaction out of cutting the grass than playing tennis." Another player who reached a career high of number six in the world and earned over three million dollars in the game in his career said to me while having lunch, "Jeff, the truth is that I never reached number one in the world, and I feel like a failure. When I realized that Irian Tiriac, Becker's coach at the time, would receive a hospitality car instead of me, I realized I was slipping." What is happening in these cases? And what can we learn from this?

In Wilander's situation, he obviously experienced a feeling of disillusionment once he arrived at the goal he had set early on. I believe he lost sight of the process along the way—the thrill of the battle in this quest—and was grossly disappointed with the value he had placed on the outcome. Once he got there, I believe he began to feel the pressure of defending something he no longer believed in or could hold on to. He realized the power he had placed in a ranking was actually empty. Also, Wilander developed a very extrinsic form of motivation, based more on the outcome, rather than on an intrinsic one—a motivation that is based on an internal sense of achievement of his goals and joy of competing. To continually improve and avoid burnout, it is critical to develop a love for growth and improvement. You can always find something to work on and improve. This mentality keeps the game fresh and helps you appreciate your success along the way.

Players who have not learned to compete with this process approach and internal standard of success tend to focus more attention on their opponents, their ranking, approval, and the next win, which invariably lead to muscle tension, frustration, and poor results.

The solution is really to embrace the process and recognize that how you compete, the commitment you make to improve your game, and how much you are able to enjoy each moment you get on the court will actually help you enjoy the game more, play better, and win more consistently. It is a paradigm shift that involves the balancing act of applying yourself toward tangible results while you appreciate the process of competing and improving.

Tiger Woods captured the essence of this mentality when he acknowledged, "Winning wasn't my goal. My goal wasn't breaking the record. My goal was to be able to play in the U.S. Open with everything on the line. That's what I set out to do. I knew if I played my game, I'd win."

To cultivate a more process-oriented mind-set, emphasize having fun again. Focus your attention on the joy you receive from simply hitting the ball, especially on important points. Then acknowledge to yourself that winning feels good to you but also that how you play and what you learn to apply in future matches are the most satisfying aspects of the game. In the end, it's all about shifting your focus to what really matters—testing yourself, putting yourself on the line, and hitting the shots you believe in with a sense of joy.

Todd Martin, formerly top ten in the world, put it this way, "Like anything else in life, we must focus on the process to get the desired result. In my case, instead of worrying about being down two sets to love, I stopped thinking about the result and started focusing my attention on each point—one point at a time. It's a cliché, but it's how you have to think." This new mentality certainly paid off for Todd. In the 2000 U.S. Open, you may remember his exciting comeback down two sets to love against Greg Rusedski and Carlos Moya, respectively.

Developing a more process-oriented mind-set requires a certain respect for life and a deeper awareness of the enjoyment that comes from the game. It takes courage to step back and look at your patterns and recognize that you may be too attached to the outcome. But once you do see it and recognize that you will not take any of your wins, trophies, or fleeting admiration that you receive with you, you can finally focus on hitting the ball with freedom.

16

Broaden Your Definition of Confidence

In my sport psychology practice, I often hear things like, "If I could just get a few matches under my belt, then I might get some confidence back." It would be difficult to go through a weekend tournament and not hear players mention confidence as a factor in their wins or losses. But if you look closely enough at the statement made above, you'll also see that confidence is perceived almost always as something that happens to players as opposed to something that is within their control. That is, winning or hitting a string of successful returns in a match are the *only* real ways to gain confidence. While there is no doubt that winning and immediate results have the most immediate impact on our confidence, we cannot overlook alternative strategies to raise the confidence meter when it drops.

If your confidence is low and you want to get back on track, recall some of your past successes. Often, your mind can get lost in what you're not doing well, particularly when you find yourself low on confidence. Reflect on your strengths and acknowledge that the fact that you have played well in the past means you can recapture a winning mindset again. You need to believe in yourself and your abilities.

Therefore, your perspective of confidence needs a slightly broader definition—one based on your overall athletic talent, ability to make important adjustments in a match, and evidence that you learn from past mistakes.

For example, let's say you've lost a string of close three-set matches in the last couple of months. And now you're up a break at 4–3 in the third set but end up losing your serve to even it at 4–4. The reality is that even after being broken, you are still even in the match at 4–4. What happened four weeks ago—or the volley you missed to lose this last game—becomes irrelevant. These results are as irrelevant as what you ate for dinner that same night four weeks ago. You simply don't give them any air time. Instead, you remember the many penetrating ground strokes that have served you well in the past, and you see these images clearly. You decide to trust your shots because you've hit them well in the past and you know your ability is still there. Even though you were just broken, you stay calm and recognize that your best stuff can come out at any time if you continue to trust and adjust as necessary. You can surely practice this mentality from one moment to the next. Off the court, review videos of yourself that remind you of times when you felt more confident. Get a journal and write down how you felt and played in past successful matches. Just don't forget that your ability is not something that comes and goes just because of a few disappointing matches. It's there, and you simply need to trust it. Avoid labeling or judging yourself too harshly and thereby convincing yourself you've lost confidence.

My recommendation is to simply get clear on what it means for you to act in a confident manner—regardless of the situation or score—and base your confidence on that. With a more composed outlook, expanded belief in your overall ability, and memories of positive past performances combined with some more wins under your belt, confidence will feel more enduring.

17

Give Yourself
Permission to Miss

Self-doubt creeps in at the worst moments. That's what makes it so irritating. Just when we need a dose of confidence the most, we are struck by waves of doubt, indecision, and fear that paralyze us. We shuffle through our Rolodex of possible shots to use on our first break point of the set—hitting a deep crosscourt return, playing aggressively as we have been doing prior to this moment, or adding some extra spin to keep the ball in. Which option to take? Too often, the answer is relatively simple: Just keep it in. Don't make any careless errors. Or, for some of us, we decide to do the exact opposite: Go for it but win the point quickly. Either way, the message is similar when self-doubt is running the show—that is, whatever you choose to do, just don't give it away. Many of us end up choosing the tentative approach. It just feels safer. After all, we think, at least our opponent has a chance of missing, too. The fact is, sometimes we scrape by and win the game—which makes this habit hard to give up—but most of the time we get punished.

Think back to the last tournament or match you played. Did you truly go for your shots? Did you find yourself worried about missing? Did you hit with authority when the score was close or just play it safe? Think about your return of your opponent's second serve; your approach to this shot can often reflect your mind-set in these situations. Often, this is a time when you can be aggressive immediately. Remember, this is a situation you work hard to create from point-to-point from the baseline, so why not take advantage of the short second serve when it is presented to you? Rarely, except at the pro level, is the second serve coming so hard that you can't occasionally take at least some offense. And if you are fortunate enough to have a weapon, there is no reason why you can't step up occasionally and dictate this shot immediately, especially if you have strong ground strokes. Why do so few players really go after this shot? I believe it's because they fear missing and giving up a "free point."

Players often tell me how much better they play when they commit to playing freely and authoritatively. You can see the difference, especially when they return an out second serve. One player described how he could do the same even on a first serve when he was that relaxed. When this player just hit away without the tension of keeping the ball in and controlling his shots so much, he would nail the ball perfectly over the net for a winner. One time when we were on the court, I approached the net and asked him how he felt when he hit that out serve. He said, "I just hit it. I wasn't even thinking. The serve looked like it might be out, so I just swung away. It felt great."

If you want to maximize your ability as a player and break through the barrier of playing tentatively and second-guessing your shots, you need to be willing to swing freely through the ball without hesitation. You need to be decisive, and if you don't feel decisive, begin acting that way. Playing it safe in any form is a recipe for disappointment, frustration, and stagnation. It takes courage to swing through the ball, especially if you aren't feeling great on a particular day, but you need to trust your ability and go for it—within your skill range. Protecting against errors *is* the problem, and choosing to move out of this restricted mind-set will help free you up so you can move to the next level. Ultimately, this decisiveness will pay off big dividends in your game and make you feel more fulfilled on and off the court.

Playing in the championship match in northern Germany in 1999, I was down 5–2 in the second set (my outcome would tie or lose the match for our team) when I recognized how my own self-doubt was preventing me from returning serve with any authority and ultimately keeping me from winning the match. In that moment, I made a decision. Instead of chipping and guiding my return of serve, I would step in and commit to hitting through it, regardless of the outcome. In my mind, going for my shots at this point was simply an investment I needed to make. So, with a renewed sense of purpose and commitment, I became a wall and simply threw my weight into the ball with authority. It worked—a winner backhand crosscourt. My confidence meter instantly rose. I did it again and hit an unreturnable forehand—I can still remember it to this day. Needless to say, this new approach won me the set and match.

I tell you this story because it was a turning point for me psychologically when I recognized the power of the mind in overcoming self-doubt on the court. I realized that we don't need to be victims of periodic doubt and can choose to play with conviction each point. The awareness, commitment, and physical energy I generated from one moment to the next are available to you, too. Next time self-doubt knocks on your door, answer with the decision to swing freely through the ball without hesitation.

18

Leave Your Expectations Off the Court

There is a big difference between striving for excellence in your game and carrying those expectations onto the court. All successful players have a very high standard for themselves; many are even perfectionists. This drive is what propels them to put in the time and endure the pain and monotony of extreme self-improvement. However, the best competitors have learned to leave their expectations off the court so they can play freely and manage the stress that comes with the unpredictability of competition.

It may seem like the pursuit of excellence and expectations go hand in hand. But they needn't. You need to accept that you won't hit every return perfectly or play flawlessly. You will make errors. You will occasionally start out slowly until you find your groove. You may lose to players ranked below you. The trajectory of your improvement rarely follows a path that goes straight up. Keep striving for personal excellence but try to suspend your expectations of how you "should" be playing when you're on the court.

You hear it all the time from players: "How could I miss that shot? I never miss that. This is a joke." It is certainly an understandable reaction. You know how you can play. And you know when you are executing your shots or not. Beware of your tendency to judge. To move beyond the self-imposed expectations, you need to recognize that comparing and judging your shots will only keep you stuck.

Tennis is a unique sport, given that it has no time limit. Amazingly, you can be down 6–0, 5–0, 4–0 and still win. You do have time to find your rhythm. You don't have to get frantic when your forehand isn't landing deep in your opponent's court like it did the day before. How well you performed and whether you fulfilled your expectations are best assessed when the match is over.

The tendency is to get down on yourself and feel disappointed that you aren't playing the way you know you can. You start thinking more about what isn't working and wonder what to do now. Your brain goes into overdrive, and you get caught in your head. Avoid this track. Stop analyzing. Refocus on the task at hand. Recall what your best strokes look like. Just accept what is and see if you can relax your body. More than likely, it is the tension in your body and your busy mind that are causing you to miss your shots in the first place—that is, unless your opponent is forcing you into new and uncomfortable situations.

For years, my own expectations caused me to obsess over lost matches for weeks. I would get unnecessarily flustered if I didn't execute a shot as I had expected. I wanted things to flow just right. Well, I know now that my expectations on the court only handcuffed me. Once I learned to withhold my judgment until I had a chance to find my groove, my best tennis did emerge.

You want to play well and win. But to do so, you need to leave your expectations off the court while you immerse yourself in the match.

19

Establish Your Presence Before Serving

Over the past ten years, I have watched adult and junior players take the most important part of the game—the serve—and dismiss it. Whether it's the impatience to get the next point started, frustration with the serve in general, anxiety about double-faulting, or just plain old habit, the actions in which players engage in the time prior to serving is perhaps the most widely abused time in the game. Establishing your presence at the line before serving will translate into a sense of confidence and an improved serving percentage.

It wasn't until I finished playing college tennis and was about six months into the pro tour that I finally woke up to the fact that my serve and my approach to it would be a deciding factor in my win/loss record. For the most part, it was impatience that got the best of me. I just was often impulsive to start the point. I wasn't centered at the line before serving. I was often caught between the meaning I was making about the last point and my irritation at my low first-serve percentage. I simply didn't understand the importance of a routine before serving.

Don't get me wrong, I wasn't totally off track. I did bounce the ball three times before serving—a routine I still use today—but I missed the other key elements, namely picturing where I was serving and making sure my arm was loose enough.

When I began using a pre-serve routine consistently, I noticed that I became looser and more focused, which seemed to add pace and consistency to my first serve. A loose arm is critical while serving, and this pre-serve routine helped me get my mind and body prepared for this opportunity to dictate the point immediately. In time, I also started getting some more "free" points on my serve (a huge bonus I hadn't fully accounted for until it started happening), and my confidence grew because I was more relaxed on my returns since I was holding easier. The following steps should help you, too.

Before serving, practice the progression of B, P, R (breath, placement, relaxed arm) as your routine. First, take a deep breath as you walk to the line to establish your presence. This is brief but deliberate. Second, create a quick visual image in your mind of the ball traveling toward your target. Make sure you are decisive with your placement of the serve. No second-guessing. This is critical. Third, check the tension in your shoulders and arm. Keep a loose arm! This routine is followed by you bouncing the ball a set number of times (how many times is up to you) and then serving. Keep this routine consistent and practice it regularly so it's automatic.

Routines help us stay confident, focused, and relaxed. The serve, particularly, requires a clear mind and loose body because it is the only shot we are initiating. If you create this mind-body combination (a loose arm with a sense of intention), you will begin seeing better results on your serve. However, don't forget to hit buckets of balls, too! These tips are not meant as a replacement for consistent practice.

20

Face Your Fears

After feeling continually disappointed with her rate of improvement and results in recent tournaments, a client confided in me, "The more you invest, the more you lose." Of course, it was her perspective that scared me the most.

I have witnessed similar beliefs among a number of players over the years. Many players might not come right out and acknowledge that they are scared of trying and failing and the pain that comes with it, but I know how fear can creep into our lives. Even if we do not recognize it as fear, it shows up in defeated body language, minimal effort in matches, tentative ground strokes, worry about the match outcome, even the tournaments we choose to play. But here's the truth: Fear isn't the real problem. The problem is the fear of the fear, the shame, disappointment, embarrassment, frustration you might experience if things don't go your way. So, rather than calling someone to play with you who might say no, you avoid it. Rather than playing a tournament where you may not do as well, you avoid it. Rather than going for your shots on break point, you play tentatively and avoid the possibility of missing. The list goes on and on. It's the avoidance of the fear that is in your way. And the only effective way to deal with this pattern is to begin facing your fears head -on.

I know you don't want to feel bad. You don't want to confirm what you secretly think may be true about you or your game. Because what if you're right? *No*, you say, *I have to avoid that situation at all costs.* You do not want to feel the anxiety when you go for it and miss, the disappointment when you lose to someone ranked below you, the rejection by another player who won't play with you. You choose to "duck" a tournament rather than risk a drop in your ranking. What is the consequence of letting fear dictate your choices? Unfortunately, you pay in unrealized potential, missed opportunities, and loss of enjoyment in the game. What's the alternative? Face your fear. Make the call to someone you want to play with, hit out on your shots, play the tournament, don't give up in matches, stand tall when things aren't going your way, practice hard, tell your partner what you need. The more you face your fear, the easier it gets, and the better you will play.

You have all the right equipment, you take lessons, you spend money on travel for tournaments, and you may have a fitness trainer to get you in physical shape. You can get the upper hand on fear. But you must first acknowledge when you are fearful and become resolved to act with courage. When you do, your confidence will rise and your game will improve. You can certainly apply this same approach off the court. The more you invest, the more you gain.

21

Play for Yourself

It's easy to get caught up in the trap of wanting to please other people with your performance and results in tournaments rather than playing for yourself. Let's be honest: It feels good to have others validate you and be impressed with your game. There's just one problem with this. You can get addicted to the praise, and it eventually starts to influence your thoughts and ultimately how you play, because you put too much pressure on yourself to win. Instead of focusing on your game plan, you then have to deal with thoughts about letting others down or losing the praise you used to enjoy. When this need gets too intense, your game can begin to falter.

To recapture the joy of the game, refocus your attention on playing the way you like to; remind yourself that it is your own sense of pride and accomplishment that matter most. At the end of the day, your opinion, goals, and standard are what give you the juice to keep playing and improving.

I often reflect on the innocent eyes of many of the ambitious yet anxious junior players I've spent time with over the years when I've suggested they start playing more for themselves. Their look is one of amazement, as if they have been waiting for someone to give them permission to play freely without the expectations of others weighing them down. When they become aware of the pressure they have been feeling and decide to let some of this go, they often play better and have more fun in the process.

One girl I worked with about two years ago had fallen in the rankings partly due to an injury and partly because she was feeling pressure to win. Her mother had said point-blank to her, "What's the point of playing unless you are going to be number one in the world?" The mother said the same thing even in my presence, so there was no censoring going on. The problem with this pressure was that this girl was not in a psychological place where that idea was even remotely helpful. She was losing matches, and that expectation was only stressing her out. She confided in me how losing was scary and embarrassing. The thought of playing girls ranked below her terrified her. She was no longer playing for herself.

In time, we focused on what she had control over and how she could turn her mother's statements into humor. She had a good sense of humor, so this was very effective. She realized how her mother's lack of experience in the game and own struggle as a child were the main reasons for the pressure she was projecting onto her daughter. With some humor and awareness, this player was able to turn things around and began playing with more confidence once she realized she was the only one who could hit the ball. She realized the pressure was not really about her.

With the exception of doubles, which of course require more compromise, to play for yourself means you recognize that playing tennis is your experience and one that you deserve to have without interference from others. You are the only one who can decide on strategy changes in the match, feel the full excitement and pressure in tournaments, and ultimately take responsibility for yourself and your game. You need to give yourself permission to play full-out and enjoy the drama of all your matches. Savor your experiences on the court and know that you are the only one who can execute your plan. This game belongs to you. You don't have to live out the needs of others.

Once you learn to play more for yourself and do the best you can, you will notice that the crowd just blends into the surroundings. You will feel a sense of independence and freedom that is self-affirming. Your confidence grows from this experience because you are no longer in need of anything outside yourself to the same degree. It's a great way to play and experience the game.

22

Focus on Your Game Plan in Tiebreakers

You've just played a long first set. Perhaps you even know that, based on statistics, if you win this one, you have an 85 percent chance of winning the match. Your heart beats a bit faster. Let's face it, if there is a time to play well, it's now. Don't let your mind run away on you just because it is a tiebreaker. Remember that your opponent is going through his own mental dance. Therefore, it's important to stay composed and not overreact.

First, there is a reason you are in a tiebreaker. You've done quite a few things right, and you need to be clear on what they are from the beginning of the tiebreaker. You may need to remind yourself to work the point, hit your forehand to their backhand, or get in your first serves to avoid having to rely on your second serve. This is not a time to do anything drastically different. Approach the first point of the tiebreaker with confidence and determination and use the shots that got you there.

Because the tiebreaker decides the entire first set, the tendency is to either go for too much too soon or play tentatively, hoping your opponent misses. In *Winning Ugly: Mental Warfare in Tennis—Lessons from a Master*, Brad Gilbert says, "Playing quickly and carelessly can immediately put you at a disadvantage from which you won't recover."

When you are composed, you will be better able to find a balance between consistency and going for your shots.

To improve your chance of winning a tiebreaker, you need to narrow your focus considerably and remind yourself to play one point, even one shot, at a time. Isolating each point in this way will help you reduce your nervous tension and keep you focused on the task at hand—a skill that becomes even more critical in a tiebreaker when tension is typically running high. If your mind wanders to the result of the set, which is normal, you need to bring it back gently to the point at hand and refocus on your strategy—ideally, the next shot.

If you recall any of the celebrated matches of our time—the Bjorn Borg versus John McEnroe Wimbledon final, the Agassi versus Sampras U.S. Open quarterfinal in 2001, the Blake versus Agassi U.S. Open quarterfinal in 2005—you will remember how composed these players looked in tiebreakers. They have learned to focus on the point at hand and seem to accept, even embrace, the noise, pressure, and enormity of the moment, regardless of the score.

The more you are able to isolate each point and be clear with your strategy, the more likely you will win the tiebreaker. It's common for players to overreact and abandon what has been working simply because they become overly aware of the score. Show your opponent that you have patience and are willing to work the point. It is your job to rein in your mind when it starts to run away on you.

As you focus more on constructing points and using the shots that helped put you in the tiebreaker, you will begin to feel more comfortable and composed.

23

Get Comfortable With Winning

With so many players worrying about whether they will lose, it probably seems preposterous to you that some people are actually frightened to win. But it's true. To play better in front of crowds and win more, get comfortable with winning.

One highly successful male college player I worked with recently shared with me his fear of being in the spotlight and raising people's expectations. He had endured a great deal of pressure and expectations from others to achieve early on in the game, coupled with the message, "It's important to be humble and not bring too much attention to yourself." Over time, this mixed message created considerable inner conflict for him. Gradually, he found himself critically paralyzed in big matches. He felt overwhelmed and self-conscious when he competed. If he won, the bar would be raised and he would feel pressure to keep the winning going. If he lost, he would feel deflated and guilty that he had disappointed his teammates. This no-win mind-set was certainly not a recipe for his best tennis.

Over a number of weeks, I helped him recognize that winning wasn't personal, it was simply a result—a result he could be proud of. He began to see the impact his beliefs were having on him. He started to separate these old beliefs that were handed down from family members from his own. Playing well and hitting through his shots were his right, and he began to give himself permission to compete, have fun, and win. He became less ambivalent about the meaning of winning and losing and focused on playing for himself.

Another female player I worked with struggled with a slightly different version of the same challenge—getting comfortable with winning. When she was beating a higher-ranked player and in a position to win, she would be bombarded by thoughts like, *I'm not supposed to be in this position; I don't deserve to win.* This player was highly sensitive to the opinions of others and feared being told that she was "lucky" and simply was uncomfortable being in the spotlight. With prompting, she began to shift the negative view she had of herself and raised her self-image as a player. She, too, learned to give herself permission to win.

If you find yourself holding back in matches because you worry that expectations will rise or that you don't deserve to be in a winning position, remind yourself that you have earned the right to be there. There is a reason why you have gotten this far, and you deserve to finish it off. It is your right and obligation to play your best, and whatever happens is meant to be.

The game of tennis teaches you a lot about your values and sense of character. You can't hide from yourself for very long in this game. Your win/loss record need not be the defining aspect of this game or your sense of self. It's not personal. Give yourself permission to hit out on your shots, shine in front of others, and win.

24

Separate Your Self-Worth From Your Performance

If you want to experience more freedom on the court, it is imperative that you recognize how your self-worth can get wrapped up in your performance results. You have to learn how to separate one from the other.

A fifteen-year-old nationally ranked player told me, "It would be so embarrassing if I lose to that girl. What will people think?" A forty-five-year-old nationally ranked player confided in me, "I just felt like everyone was staring at me. I was nervous to just be on the court with some of the other higher-ranked players." A current world-ranked player on the Association of Tennis Professionals (ATP) Tour shares with me how self-conscious he gets when playing in front of crowds out of fear of double-faulting. In an interview in *Inside Tennis*, prior to her comeback, Jennifer Capriati admitted that this inability to separate her self-worth from tennis was a big part of her downfall as a player. "I wanted to reach my true potential," she said, "but I wasn't doing that. I had a lot of other stuff going on, like the fears. … At one point, I was even afraid of playing in front of a crowd again. It seemed so intimidating to have people watching. A lot of it's about self-esteem … but now I've learned to differentiate how I feel about myself and what I'm doing on the court. For a long time, I didn't know how to do that." Once Capriati realized how her self-worth was getting attached to her experience on the court, she started to play the best tennis of her life.

This can be tricky, of course, because whenever we put energy into something and care about the results, our sense of self-worth can get wrapped up in it pretty quickly. The key is in recognizing that your results in tennis will provide you with some transitory satisfaction, but the real joy is in competing and playing the way you believe you can.

To begin making this shift, you need to first take stock of your reaction when you lose. Is it extremely difficult to let go and move on? It's helpful to begin observing the kinds of thoughts you are truly having. How upset do you get? Are you beating yourself up and concluding that you are inferior? Do you feel shame for losing and stew over what others might be thinking of you? If so, you are probably attaching your self-esteem to your tennis performance.

Once I caught this tiger by the tail, I started to develop a wider perspective of the game and myself. Instead of viewing each loss as a life sentence, I began to see my tennis career and performance as a process of learning and unimaginable self-discovery. Though I still wanted to win as badly as the next guy, my energy began to shift. I started feeling free, released from the handcuffs I had placed on myself when I was living in a world of comparison and anxiety.

It's important to recognize that the only real goal you need to have is learning about yourself and figuring out what factors help you play your best tennis. You need to see that the real joy is about breaking free from the chains you've placed on yourself. It's important to play with passion and react in a way you feel good about. You will not gain more worth as a person or player whether you win or lose. You may think you do, but you don't. You would be surprised how little other people are actually thinking about you and cherishing your latest win or lamenting your recent loss.

I suggest that you base your self-worth on your ability to adjust and improve, the effort you put in, and your ability to dig down when the going gets tough. Tapping into your fighting spirit and loving the battle brings a lot of satisfaction. After all, what's the downside? The reality is you will play better anyway. By keeping your results and performance confined to the court, you will be able to play more relaxed and freely. The truth is that tennis is one of the greatest teachers to help you grow both as a player and as a person.

Remind yourself that this tennis is only a game. It is an opportunity to test yourself and improve, but it is not a reflection of who you are. You are more than your ranking or a good backhand. Don't diminish yourself to a ranking or a level in the game.

25

Create Your Ideal Intensity Level

First, it's important to understand intensity, which is defined as having an extreme degree of force or energy. Regulating intensity so that it works for you is critical. Too much of it causes you to overhit and "muscle the ball"; not enough of it results in poor footwork and "flat performances."

Therefore, the key is to know how much intensity is best for you and then to train it. The first step is to develop awareness of your *current* intensity level, which you will notice by observing the force with which you hit the ball and how you walk between points when you are playing your best. Do you walk with a sense of purpose and intention?

When you are playing with the right amount of intensity, you should feel it. You approach the line with authority. You take your time. You are decisive. You look as though you are in control. You feel like you belong. You are committed to the next shot and next point.

Playing with intensity has a sense of intentionality to it. You are playing with resolve and determination. You are committed to playing the shots you know you can hit, and you choose to accept the consequences. You recognize the importance of "showing up" with a purpose.

To train this state of mind, you can also practice using a numbering system from 1 to 10, with 10 being the most intense for you and 1 being the most passive. Once you find your ideal level (most players choose between 7 and 10), you can then practice hitting the ball at this ideal level and checking in with your body after points, drills, or rallies to compare the result of your shot with the level of intensity you feel. You should begin getting more aware of your footwork and the energy needed to hit an aggressive ball and how this level of intensity corresponds to the depth and pace of your shots.

In matches, you can raise your intensity level between points by hopping on your toes, quickening your pace with a sense of renewed purpose, or exhaling as you hit the ball with more force. If you have too much intensity, and you are rushing or tightening up, you need to become aware, slow things down, remind yourself to stay calm, and take a deep "reset" breath. The improved body awareness you develop in practice will help you access your ideal state quickly, which is key when you are in competition.

When you step up to return serve or serve for the match, decide to play with intensity. Choose your shot and hit it with authority. Your willingness to play in this way, regardless of the outcome, will build up your confidence because you are committed to playing the way you know you can. This decision will improve your shot making and produce more wins, which ultimately will fuel your feeling of confidence. It starts with the decision to act with intensity and intention, even when you don't feel like it.

26

Go Out of Your Comfort Zone

It's 4–4 in the first set, and you hear the player on the next court scream, "I never miss that shot!" Immediately, you empathize. You've been there yourself—missing shots you routinely make, especially in practice. The truth is, we have all been there—in a tournament, tightening up on the "big" points, perhaps worried about the result of the match, and trying to find that feeling we had just a day or two earlier in practice. What is behind this agonizing experience, and how can you play in tournaments like you do in practice?

Transitioning from lessons to tournaments typically presents the greatest challenge and frustration for many players. Again, due to players' emphasis on winning, they are often unwilling to go out of their comfort zone long enough to witness the improvement. At the first sign of "failure" (errors), players bail out, reverting to what is comfortable. However, often their "old" shots are no longer what they used to be, either. Players will find themselves in no-man's-land within their own development—they haven't quite developed the new shots, and their old shots are "under construction."

To get beyond this frustrating no-man's-land, the first thing you can do is to think more long-term. Ask yourself if you are committed and patient enough to make the change, and even willing to risk losing some matches with the goal of greater improvement in the future. For some players, this decision will propel you to the next level almost immediately. You will find that you have given yourself permission to play freely, and this alone will be the key to your own breakthrough in tournaments. For others, it will be a more gradual climb with some possible losses along the way. You simply need to get more comfortable executing the shots you have been avoiding.

As each match becomes less threatening and is viewed as a stepping-stone to better tennis in the future, risk and nerves become less of a factor, which may be the more relevant issues in the first place. "Players get too caught up in the pure results of the tournament," said Tom Gullikson, former Davis Cup captain. "Players must be more honest with themselves, assess their strengths, and be aware of how they are reacting to pressure in tournaments. Pete Sampras would do this consistently from year to year, even in his sixth straight year as the number-one player in the world."

Simulating match play in practice can also be enormously beneficial. Many top college and pro players have acknowledged how their preparation in practice can make all the difference. "When I practiced with Aaron Krickstein," said Joey Rive, former National Junior coach for USA Tennis, who reached a career high of number fifty-seven in the world in singles, "I remember practicing as though we were already in the tournament. In our mind, by the time we played the first round of a tournament, we had already won a few rounds. This type of intensity in practice can make a huge difference for players."

Raising your intensity in practice to effectively prepare for pressure in tournaments takes creativity and a plan. Before a tournament, I often would imagine a crowd watching me while I played a tiebreaker. This would help me build the intensity and make it feel more real. The more you place yourself into pressure situations, the better. Practice serving out a set with only one serve. Have people come out and watch you play a tiebreaker and try to distract you. Make a rule that you lose points when you hit short. You have lots of options if you get creative. Practice playing aggressively on game points in practice matches. When you do this on a regular basis and maintain this as a goal in practice, you will be more likely to do this in tournaments. The more familiar you are with a specific shot or style of play, the more confident you will be in tournaments. What does this process demand of you? It takes an awareness of what will make the biggest difference for you in tournaments and that you then practice this. Which shot do you hold back from hitting in tournaments yet you know would make a huge difference if you tried it more? When you get clear on the goal or shots you know you need to hit in tournaments, you should integrate these continually in your practice sessions. Then put on your hat of courage and commit to your game plan. Don't abandon your game plan in tournaments at the first sign of danger. Stick it out and remember that your willingness to go out of your comfort zone will pay off in the long haul.

27

Narrow Your Focus in the Warm-Up

"I just couldn't get a rhythm." "From the beginning, I never felt like I was even in the match." Statements such as these show how many players feel they often start matches slowly. They are frustrated that it takes them a few games (sometimes even a set) before they feel like they are competing well. I believe the warm-up is a very important opportunity to get your feel and prepare yourself before the first point begins.

As you walk onto the court, perhaps you feel some nerves. Or maybe you are distracted by your opponent, the conditions, the draw, or who might be watching. Whatever may be taking your focus away from the moment at hand, the warm-up is an opportunity to narrow your focus and establish your rhythm immediately.

The best way to do this is by tracking the ball closely as it travels over the net and breathing purposely as you follow through after contact. This process will improve your reaction time and keep your mind calm and focused. Each time you hit the ball, you simply need to bring your focus back to the ball and exhale softly after contact.

Again, this will help you focus on something other than who you are playing and will prevent you from worrying about any excess nerves. This process resembles Tim Gallwey's approach in the 1970s when he introduced the technique of "bounce-hit" in his best-selling book *The Inner Game of Tennis* as a way to stop your mind from judging your performance.

However, what I found was that using my breath had an even greater impact on my mind and body because it slowed my respiration and relaxed my nervous system while I tuned in to the ball. This process helped me narrow my attention, which is what I needed to feel and play my best. Interestingly, the ball-breath approach also helped me access a deeper state of trust in my shots as I became more absorbed in the moment and fully connected to my body. Gradually, my confidence would start to grow. For me, getting my attention into this more narrow focus has been so helpful because my mind has a tendency to race when I am nervous, and I am very sensitive to my surroundings. By exhaling as I hit the ball and focusing on the ball more deeply, I created a kind of cocoon that insulated me from my environment. Many top players in the game today will talk about the same "cocoon-like" experience when they are in the zone.

Next time you play a match, try to take your attention and narrow it to your breath and the ball. See if you can lose yourself in the moment by tracking the ball more closely. When your opponent steps up to the line to serve, focus your eyes on the ball. This should help you override any judgmental thoughts, because you are focusing your attention on something "relevant." You will also be surprised how much you can actually pick up about your opponent because you are in a more relaxed and focused state and not thinking as much. It's amazing how much more open and perceptive you can be when you turn down the volume on your left-brain, analytical mind. Use the warm-up to get yourself into the zone and you will experience a new dimension to the game and your own ability to create the state of mind-body you need to play your best.

28

Talk About Skill
Development, Not Potential

As I walked out of my office after a session with a seventeen-year-old ranked junior, I found myself cornered by the player's father. "How did it go?" he asked overly enthusiastically. "Fine," we both said, hoping the father would not probe further. Unfortunately, he continued. For the next five minutes, he commented on his daughter's game and must have used the word *potential*—that she wasn't yet fulfilling—at least a dozen times. He also tied this to her ranking. As my client's face grew redder and redder, I shuddered to myself at the damage he was unwittingly doing in front of my eyes. In the mind of this player and virtually every other athlete I've met with over the past ten years, the word *potential* has become a ticking time bomb. I've seen players literally shrink in front of me, tank matches, even quit the sport because of the pressure they feel to achieve this intangible level of "potential."

Naturally, the session with this young player consisted of a discussion of how she could minimize the pressure she was feeling about winning or losing and the excess focus on rankings. Not surprisingly, her mind would get distracted by thoughts related to the consequence of winning, how it would help her get into college, and fulfill her mom and dad's expectations.

As the dad and my client walked out of my office, he appeared to not yet be fully satisfied and added, "Well, maybe we'll have something 'good' to report after the tournament this weekend."

The problem with labeling yourself or others with unfulfilled potential and connecting this to rankings is that there is no way to know whether you are ever there. Not only that, but given our propensity to raise the bar whenever we reach a goal, there is rarely a lasting sense of satisfaction. Thinking about potential is simply dangerous territory. It diminishes conversations about skill development and mental toughness and, in the mind of the player, leaves this huge gap between where they are right now and where they are "supposed" to be. From my experience, it's been far more crippling than productive.

Richard Williams, father of Venus and Serena, kept the two girls away from junior tennis because he didn't want to create any limitations in the way they viewed themselves as players based on early rankings. He wanted them to think bigger than a number before they fully developed. He wanted them to believe in themselves as champions and develop their game for the long haul, much like Pete Sampras, who demonstrated this by switching from a two-handed to a one-handed backhand early in his career. Sampras's long-term vision and desire to reach his potential speaks for itself.

An alternate track is to immerse yourself in the developmental process. Be curious about your progress and what you are learning. There is already so much emphasis and focus on the outcome and potential—yet to be realized—that conversations about the process of learning and improvement mixed in with achievement is a more balanced and productive path to take.

To think more long-term, focus on specific goals you can work on. Avoid comparing yourself to others. Focus on exactly the things in your game that you can improve day to day and week to week. Remember your strengths and work on your weaknesses.

Talent and athletic ability are important, but just because you may strike the ball well in practice doesn't mean you will necessarily translate this into competition. You need to be aware that your ability to manage thoughts and emotions related to winning and losing will determine your long-term growth as a player.

When you finish a tournament, try to focus on what you learned. How did you react under pressure? How aggressively did you play? Did you focus on your game plan? What do you need to work on before the next tournament? Avoid making sweeping negative judgments about your game that are more focused on ranking and comparisons of how much potential you feel you have versus your ability to consistently improve.

29

Develop Positive Chemistry With Your Doubles Partner

In virtually every seminar I have given on the mental game, players never fail to raise the question about how to handle the embarrassment, frustration, and self-sabotage they experience in doubles matches. "What should I do when I start worrying about my partner?" they ask. As I probe further, they confide in me that they worry about being rejected by their partner, dropped off the team, or simply looked down upon by peers. Professional players are not immune to similar worries in the heat of battle when they feel they are not holding up their side of the court. However, this mind-set and psychological tug-of-war can wreak havoc on your game, not to mention your enjoyment. Creating a game plan to manage this self-defeating pattern can help you avoid what I call the "codependent trap."

Based on research of doubles teams, conducted by Jim Loehr over the past decade, what has become apparent is that most professional doubles players spend approximately 75 percent more time than amateur players in matches engaging in either verbal or nonverbal communication. Often, you can see this when they join together at the service line to discuss their plan for the next point, when they tap their racquet strings in an attempt to support and motivate themselves and their partner before returning serve. Good chemistry is created with a plan, and it requires some discussion of what you like and don't like in terms of interaction and feedback from your partner. Ideally, this communication should happen well before the match and usually does for players who play with one another on a regular basis. For many league players, this type of communication often isn't possible due to the impromptu nature of their matches. Therefore, it is critical to become aware of your needs on the court so you can initiate this with your partner, at the very least, as the match unfolds. How much talking do you like? When is it helpful to you? Do you like positive encouragement when you find yourself in a rough patch, or would you rather figure it out on your own? What are your personal goals for the match?

It is important to become aware of what helps you play your best so you can create the kind of partnership that is supportive, motivating, and effective. Don't hesitate because you are worried about your partner's reaction. She will be far more irritated when it comes out anyway during the match!

Having a team mantra can be useful, too. When the going gets tough, it is helpful to have a saying that keeps you both on track. Some of my favorite sayings are, "Let's rip away and see what happens." "Ready to have some fun?" "We're not out of this yet; let's keep fighting." You may also want to have your own personal phrase that keeps your mind from straying over to the worries about what your partner is thinking (i.e., *I'm doing the best I can.*

Stay loose and go for your shots.). This type of communication needs to be only a few seconds. It doesn't take long. But the positive emotions that come out of it are well worth it. Typically, this would include a brief discussion of strategy or a motivational comment. You would be surprised what consistent communication can do for you and your partner. It makes you feel connected and not so alone, which can help minimize your negative self-talk and stop your codependent behavior on the court.

30

Don't Let Your Emotions Run the Show

It's natural to assume that if you have feelings of low confidence, anxiety, or anger, you can't do anything about it. Many people feel that emotions are simply part of their make-up. In the world of cognitive psychology, it's called emotional reasoning—that is, we label ourselves based on our emotions. However, in reality, just because you feel a certain way doesn't mean it is true.

One player I work with lacks confidence in tournaments but plays incredibly well in practice. Literally, she is like two different players. This problem has been going on for the past three or four years mainly because she hasn't ever entertained the idea that her feeling of insecurity is caused by her thoughts in the first place. Helping her recognize that her negative, irrational thoughts can, in fact, be changed has paved the way for new emotions to emerge.

Because thoughts happen in our mind so quickly, without self-monitoring or observing our thinking patterns, we can become entrenched in negative emotions that actually have very little validity. The key is to begin checking in with yourself when you notice you are feeling anxious or down about your game. Usually, if you pay attention, you will be able to notice that your mind has taken a turn down the negative track: *I am so sick of practicing. I hope I play well today. I have not been feeling good on the court lately.* The thoughts come quickly, but you should gradually be able to catch yourself thinking negative thoughts when you notice that a particular emotion has descended upon you.

My client recently went out and won a string of three-set matches, having faced multiple match points in her tournament and ended the season number one in her conference. Once she realized that she didn't need to be victimized by her feelings and that she had a choice over what she could think at any given moment, she stopped labeling herself as a player who had no confidence. Be careful of the labels. Our emotions are not always based on the truth.

Next time you notice you are feeling low on confidence, panicky, angry, or impatient, ask yourself, *What am I thinking right now?* Once you identify the thought or stream of thoughts, ask yourself if what you are thinking is, in fact, true. Ask yourself if there might be another perspective. There is always an alternative perspective that is available if you take a moment to challenge what you are thinking.

31

Develop Emotional and Physical Flexibility

As you'll see throughout this book, there are many doorways that can help you play better and become more emotionally and physically flexible; you will then find your game and results improve dramatically. My favorite suggestion is to try yoga.

The truth is, before I actually tried yoga, I had been thinking about it for a couple of years. Deep down, I knew that slowing down like this for over an hour would be incredibly challenging. But five years ago, I decided to test my patience and walked into a local gym for a class. In the first class, I felt distracted, impatient, and frustrated that I couldn't do the poses properly. Although I felt like bolting out of the class multiple times, I stuck it out and finished the class. I was proud of myself. And I went back the next week. I got a little more comfortable with the movements the following week and was determined to finish the class, which I did. After about four weeks, I was hooked.

What was the result? I became more patient. I improved my ability to stay focused. I felt mentally calmer for at least two days afterward.

On the court, I know it paid off. My breathing patterns improved, and I could access this calmer state more easily than before.

The research is relatively new on yoga, but it is starting to show dramatic results in lowering blood pressure, calming the autonomic nervous system, and positively impacting your brain's neurochemistry.

There is probably no better way to practice your emotional, mental, and physical flexibility than yoga. It will test your will and help you become more aware of how active your mind is. Learning to calm your mind and overcome passing frustration in yoga will help you manage the difficult moments on the court with more grace.

Of course, taking the step into the yoga room for the first time may be your biggest challenge. But once you do, you may find an activity that can profoundly impact your tennis game and your life.

32

Smile to Expand Your Perspective

Have you ever noticed that smiling or laughing makes you feel better? Thanks to your brain's neurochemistry, you can actually alter the way you feel by smiling. A smile can increase the serotonin in your brain—one of the important chemicals responsible for your sense of optimism and enjoyment. If you find yourself in a rough patch on the court, trying hard to fix your strokes and get your game back, with no success, you may want to try smiling to expand your perspective in the moment.

Many players will respond to a series of poorly executed shots by overthinking their technique. As you try harder, you can often make matters worse. The harder you try, the more self-conscious and frustrated you become. To improve your chances of getting back on track and improving your mood, try smiling at yourself and the situation. It is likely that you are taking the situation too seriously and aren't giving your body a chance to find a rhythm.

Five years ago, I was playing in the second round of qualifying at the Siebel Open, a 500k ATP tournament in San Jose, California.

Playing against a former NCAA Champion eleven years my junior, with numerous coaches and other players sitting on the sidelines, I certainly had some adrenaline shooting through my body. I was also injured with a sprained ankle from the week before, which was well wrapped.

Although I was feeling somewhat tense, I prepared myself to return serve for the first point of the match. Ace. Next point. Ace. In a matter of about one minute I was aced four times! That had never happened to me in my twenty-five years in the game as a competitive player.

As I walked over to exchange ends and grab my towel, I was a bit shell-shocked. *What if this match is a blowout? How will I ever compete with a serve like that?* But rather than stew over this and examine my return of serve too closely, I remember spontaneously smiling to myself, which immediately lightened up the situation. Interestingly, it helped me find some helpful perspective in the moment.

To my surprise, the smile helped just enough to keep me out of my head. I rattled off the next six out of seven games, breaking him twice to win the set. Rather than trying too hard or going for too much to compensate for the embarrassing first game, I was able to step back and stay focused on playing one point at a time and let my body do what it knew how to do.

I didn't always react to difficult moments on the court like this. I know how frustrating it is to be off your game and unable to get things back on track. But I also know that too much effort can be counterproductive and that expanding your view is a more productive path to take.

You often see players smile like this when everything seems to be going against them. It's an instinctive response when a situation seems overwhelming. Whether you're aced four times a game, get a series of bad line calls, or feel the wheels coming off, look up and smile. You may find that elevating your mood and stepping back from the situation with a little humor is all you need to get your rhythm and momentum back.

33

Keep Your Cool When the Bad Line Call Happens

It couldn't come at a worse time. You're on the verge of securing your lead or about to win the match when your opponent calls your ball out. You're convinced the ball hit the line, and you come unglued. But if you don't want to hand over the momentum to your opponent, you may want to rethink this situation. Your reaction in this moment could determine who walks off with the balls and a win.

In my quarter of a century in the game, I've seen players come to blows, parents issued warnings by the police, and teams threaten their opponents—all over a bad line call. Let's be honest. Given the time and energy you put into the game, it's agonizing to be cheated. It makes the hair on your neck stand up. It ignites the fight-or-flight part of your brain to go into attack mode. I understand.

However, if you want to get the upper hand on this situation, you may want to ask yourself at what cost are you losing your temper? What typically happens to your game as the stress hormones invade your nervous system?

This issue has been a consistent source of confusion and frustration for hundreds of players I've talked with over the years. What should you do? Stay cool. It's not personal. Your opponent probably did see the ball out, even if only because they needed to see it that way. If it's a big point, and you want to challenge the call, you need to stay calm, walk up to the net, and say, "I'm hoping for a fair match. Would you consider taking two on that?" Appealing to your opponent's guilty conscience is probably your best option to get the call reversed.

If you don't want to try to help your opponent "save face" and reverse the call, I highly suggest that you pause immediately after the "bad" line call and take a good deep breath. Once you are composed, remind yourself that your opponent is probably feeling the heat and is scared, which is why he is making this bad line call. Yes, he wants to win, but he's also scared. Then take any leftover frustration and use it to play better. Step up your game, begin dictating play, and stay aggressive. Show your opponent that you are still in charge and will not be swayed by the call, as if to say, "You shouldn't have done that." Get your game face back on. Remember that this call will not determine the outcome of the match, but your attitude will. Keep your momentum. Don't let your opponent steal that from you as well as the last point. The route you choose is up to you.

34

Don't Fall Into the Negative-Filtering Trap

You want to improve, play better in tournaments, and win more. The quest up the ladder of success—the position on the team, your ranking, and status among peers—are all within reach. However, beware. The gap between where you are now and achieving your goal could reside in how you are interpreting your success and setbacks along the way. Be careful of the negative-filtering trap.

Occasionally, I will get on the court with players to see how they play in point situations. I want to see how they construct points, handle mistakes, and carry themselves between points. It gives me an important glimpse into a player's mind-set and approach to the game. One client I worked with for three years called me because he was unable to kick the habit of extreme self-sabotage and anger on the court. When he would miss a ball, almost without exception, the racquet would hit the ground or the fence; sometimes he would even loft it over the fence (one time narrowly missing an older woman in a wheelchair moving past the court). The amazing thing about this particular player was that even on his best days—when we had deep, hard-hitting eight- to ten-ball rallies—and he would miss a ball, he would get visibly disgusted with himself.

One day, after one of these rallies, I walked up to the net and said, "That was one of the best rallies we've ever had. What were you thinking when you missed that last ball?"

"I should have gone back crosscourt," he said, exasperated. "You'd think by now I'd be able to hit a simple ball down the line. How idiotic can you get?"

The reality that this player had hit eight clean, penetrating, deep shots side to side was totally unacknowledged. It was lost in his mental-filtering system. There wasn't any room for positive success whatsoever.

Getting stuck in the negative-filtering trap can be deadly. After a while, you begin to actually seek out proof that you aren't good enough, consistent enough, or fast enough. The mind has decided that you are simply not where you *should* be, and you beat yourself up for it constantly.

To combat this trap, you need to, once again, tune in to your thinking pattern. You need to ask yourself if there is anything positive about what is happening at the same time. Your mind will probably tend to minimize your accomplishments, but you need the other part of your brain to enter the debate and point out things you did well. I cannot tell you how many examples there are of players coming off the court with a distorted view of their game. One player I worked with lost a match 7–6, 6–4, and told me that it was the worst match he ever played. He could not find one positive thing he did well. This mind-set was a huge obstacle in his development because he tended to react negatively on the court after any error. Eventually, he learned to see his game from a slightly more balanced perspective. This is not a recipe simply to accept mediocrity or some Pollyannaish view on your life or game. It's an act of keeping the ledger balanced.

To the observing eye, tennis is, as are most sports, pretty black and white. If the ball lands inside the white lines more than your opponent's, you win. If not, you lose. You walk off the court, and people ask, "How did you do?" You answer: "I won" or "I lost." Black and white. However, what is *really* happening is so much more. With every defeat, there will be mini successes and things you learned that could propel you forward in your next match or even be a turning point in your career, if you see it that way.

When you find yourself stuck on the negative path, tune in to your thoughts and examine the evidence. If you're fair, you will most likely find a few positive examples of your greatness.

35

Treat Sitters With the Same Intensity as Other Shots

I cannot tell you how many players have battled with the "sitter"—you know, that floating ball that seems to hang in the air for minutes when you're at net or a midcourt ball that makes you salivate at the opportunity of finishing off the point. These situations are enough to make you want to pull your hair out. However, you don't need to get the "yips" just because the ball is placed exactly where you want it. The key lies in your ability to treat the "sitter" ball with the same intensity you would hit any other shot.

It's true that you have a lot more time for your mind to do back-flips when you are presented with this opportunity. You instantly see these situations as ones in which you *should* execute. After all, you have worked hard for this moment, either through some aggressive, well-placed shots or your opponent's mistake, and it is time to cash in. So, within milliseconds, your mind essentially sends the message, *Don't miss this one. This is the opportunity you've been waiting for.* In response to that pressure, your intensity rises, causing your muscles to tighten up—even if just slightly—and you pull your eye off the ball, you peek to see where it might land, and you pray that you didn't do what you were most afraid of. Then the frustration sets in, perhaps even a dose of self-consciousness to remind you to protect against this happening again if such a shot is handed to you on a silver platter. Of course, there is always the added challenge of having to generate your own pace, which can also increase your tension level and cause you to muscle the ball.

I will never forget the match while I was in juniors when my opponent won the first set and was leading 17–16 in the second-set tiebreaker. On match point, he came into the net on a deep approach shot; I ran down a ball, barely floating a defensive shot to his forehand side for an easy put-away volley while I crashed into the side curtain and went down to the ground. Wide-eyed, I sat and watched as he hit the "sitter" volley into the back curtain to even the score at 17–17. My opponent was demoralized, and I went on to win the tiebreaker and the third set 6–0. As is so often the case in these situations, my opponent simply had too much time to think and couldn't decisively put the ball away.

The good news is that, with a minor shift of your mental approach, you can become a master of short balls and sitters and knock them away with precision and confidence. In fact, simply acknowledging the fact that you may be treating these types of situations differently can help you minimize their impact in the future. What you want to do is become aware of the intensity that you like most when you are hitting your shots confidently and with authority. You will want to notice the energy in your body and how loose you are when you are hitting your shots well. Then you simply need to drop into this state when you are running to that sitter ball, which you certainly have time for. I have found that treating the sitter ball as any other shot helps the most. Acting decisively and focusing your attention on the ball can help you maintain the proper intensity. It's a sort of matter-of-fact attitude that you need.

Next time you are faced with the sitter, stay even-keeled and approach it with the same intensity and watch your execution and confidence with these shots rise.

36

Ignore Your Inner Critic

How could you miss that shot, you idiot? This is going to be another bad day. So goes your inner critic. Don't feel bad. You're not alone. Players at all levels have to learn how to manage their negative dialogue. It's understandable. We grew up listening to parents, coaches, and peers telling us how we should do things differently or better. To add fuel to our self-incriminating fire, we live in a success-oriented culture, which makes us second-guess our achievement, fear failure, and compare ourselves to others constantly. If your inner critic is running the show, you may be listening too closely.

We see the critic working its spell on all kinds of players. Goran Ivanisevic was famous for his bloodcurdling screams when he would lose a point; Marat Safin is noted for destroying more racquets than anyone can count. What is happening when all reason and rationale are thrown out the window? And how do we get a handle on this slippery critic, also commonly referred to as our ego?

In chapter thirty, I introduced the idea of not believing every emotion you have as being an accurate reflection of the facts. Getting clear on the truth can be helpful in these instances. However, there is another strategy that may be helpful for you when your inner critic is highly active. Become aware of your thoughts and learn to detach from them. To do this, ask yourself, *What was I just saying to myself?* Once you get used to catching the thought, you can begin to make a choice whether you are going let it derail you and your performance. You will begin noticing more and more what you are saying to yourself. Then let the thoughts pass by without engaging with them or reacting to them. This strategy is not about changing your thoughts (that can be useful, too, as I've pointed out, depending on you and the particular situation). This is about detaching from your thoughts and letting them pass by before they take you down into the negative spiral. You will want to practice this off the court first to get better at this process.

Last year I was working with a former world-ranked doubles player immediately prior to Wimbledon. He reported to me that he was worried about playing poorly and letting his doubles partner down in front of spectators. He explained to me that this had happened in the past, and he had some "scar tissue" around it. In the middle of matches, he would have thoughts like, *You're going to blow it again. He'll never want to play with you again, and your ranking is going to drop.* Through our work, this player began to recognize his own thoughts—the process of identifying and articulating them provided great relief for him almost immediately. He learned to flush his thoughts down the toilet when they were emerging in his mind. By doing this, he had the mental room to focus on his strategy and felt less victimized by the negative thoughts.

The key is to understand that your mind's job is to produce lots of thoughts, ideas, and solutions. It is always trying to work something out, and it's no different on the court. The mind wants to fix errors, avoid double-faults, get rid of even the hint of nervous energy. All this mental energy is really counterproductive and un-necessary. But that's what your mind has been trained to do. So stop taking your thoughts so seriously. Let them go once in a while and make choices on the court that you feel reflect the highest value you hold of yourself and your game.

37

Get Out of Your Head on Break Points

Regardless of your level, converting break-point opportunities is a skill every player can improve upon. Understandably, break points can raise your heart rate and cause you to overthink the situation, taking you out of the moment and into a tentative mode. To improve your conversion rate on break points, you need to get out of your head.

In 2003 when I was playing the best tennis of my life and thinking about returning to the pro tour for a year to test my game and newfound mental clarity, I happened to be practicing with a player currently on the pro tour. He knew I was a sport psychology consultant, and at the end of practice, he turned to me and asked, "So do you have any suggestions for me?"

"About what?" I asked.

"I just can't seem to get the breaks," he said with his head down. "I am so close. I've lost a string of matches in the last six months that, had I won, I would be in the top hundred by now. It's not that I'm playing that tight or anything. I'm just not winning them. I tell myself to go for it. Maybe I'm not breathing enough," he admitted. "I don't know. It's just really frustrating."

Relating to this player's frustration and desire to do well, to achieve his dream of really making it on the pro tour, I do admit that I was thinking to myself, *I wish I could give him a magic bullet to fix this, to help him break out of this pattern.* But, having gone through a similar process in my own career, and with many clients with whom I've worked, I know that players need to learn more about exercising personal choice and feeling more empowered within their own minds, within themselves. This shift, as I learned over the years, given this type of in-the-moment pressure, requires a slightly more balanced perspective coupled with an individualized strategy or response that means something to him. So what did I tell him? "Forget the techniques on this one," I said, hoping to empower him more fully, as a real person with real feelings and a sense of self-control. "How about just getting out of your head completely when you are in this situation?" Then I asked, "How much pressure are you really feeling on these points when you reflect on it right now?"

He looked down for a moment to ponder my question and with some hesitancy looked up at me and like a waterfall it came pouring out. "A lot, I guess. You know, I'm just so close to being in the top hundred. If only I could win these matches, then …," His voice trailed off. He stopped in midsentence and cracked a slight smile—as if to say, "I see what you are saying."

"So getting out of the world of thought altogether might not be a bad idea, now, would it?" Pointing to the ball under the chair, I said, "See that ball? Focus your attention on it. Now look at the fuzz from the ball on your racquet strings. Then focus on the naval area of your stomach with your mind and let your mind just drop down out of your head and into your body." I continued with him and had him move his attention into his arms, legs, and face. He did all of this successfully.

Gradually a smile came to his face. "So you're saying I can shift my focus anytime I want?" he confirmed with enthusiasm.

"That's right. We choose what we focus our attention on. In your case, it seems as though you are still very much in your head when you're faced with what you call 'a big point.' So I'm wondering how this might feel for you to focus your attention more within your body to relax, watch the tension disappear if it's there, and accept whatever shows up. Instead of focusing on the score, shift your attention to the joy of being there and how good you feel, again in your body—embracing the moment, thriving on it."

Intrigued, he said, "I see what you mean. I'm not really forcing myself to do anything differently. I'm just shifting my attention in a relaxed way. I have control over what I do with my mind."

"The zone never lies," I told him as we walked off the court.

38

Let Go of the Last Point

Losing points, particularly on unforced errors, is one of the most frustrating aspects of the game. It can bring up feelings of disappointment, anger, despair, and self-doubt. You want to win the point and are acutely aware of the score. Within seconds, your mind gets caught in the vicious cycle of "what could have been" if only you had won the last point. Perhaps it would have given you a break point or an opportunity to serve out the first set. Or worse, it was match point, and you now wonder whether you can actually close this match out. Whatever the score, it is irrelevant; you need to let it go and move on to the next one. Yes, I know, easier said than done. But, armed with the right strategies, you can learn to get the upper hand on this universal mind trap.

In my CD audio program *FearlessTennis*, I shared one of my most dramatic and revealing conversations that I had with a young player about the cause of his disintegration after a match he played. In this particular match, after just the first game—of which he wasn't even serving—he became angry at himself and threw in the towel and lost 6–3, 6–2. Losing points was simply unacceptable and scary.

Let me share with you what this player said to me after the match. After he cooled down, I asked, "What were you thinking after the first game?"

"I was worried I wouldn't play well," he responded.

Challenging him, I probed further. "And what if you didn't play well?"

"Well," he said, "then I'd probably lose."

"And what if you would lose?" I continued.

"I might not get into a good college or get a good job," he said.

Finally, he acknowledged that he might even be living on the street one day!

With this kind of pressure, no technique will be very effective in wiping away the last point. So first you need to know that no match will determine the direction of your life. Even when college scholarships are on the line, college coaches are more concerned with your ability, work ethic, discipline, personality, and mental toughness. The result is not as important as you are probably making it out to be. Stay rational about it and keep it in perspective.

You also need to recognize that you will lose points, even "important" points, and you need to accept this before you walk onto the court. Even the greatest players in the game lose games, sets, and matches. They're human. So are you. If you want to increase your chances of winning, wipe away the last point. To do this, tell yourself, *It's only one point. This won't determine the match. Next point.* Or, if you doubt that you can win because you lost the last point, tell yourself, *I'm still in this. I can do it.*

It may sound simple, but these words can be extremely uplifting at crunch time. The key is to be quick and ready to go with these positive statements before your self-doubt and frustration set in.

When I was playing the ITF 35 World Championships in 2001, even though I got my mind under control before the match for the most part, I still bumped up against negative thoughts after some key points. I remember serving at 6–4, 1–0, and missing an easy forehand. Instantly the thought hit me, *What if I lose this? I'm so close.* In that moment—I still don't know how this image came to me—but I pictured a windshield wiper in my mind, wiping away the last error. Just like that, it was erased, behind me. The decks were cleared. I was free to move onto the next point and stopped stewing over the last error and assessing what it might mean. This visual has worked for many players who need a reminder to let go of the last point.

Don't let errors take you away from the match. With the right perspective, a few uplifting words, and a windshield-wiper image, you are equipped to redirect your mind when it gets pulled into the whirlpool of negativity.

39

Channel Your Anger

I have frequently been asked whether some anger in competition is normal, if not positive. The key is learning how to place your ego on the shelf and channel your energy effectively.

While some anger has proven to actually improve performance in specific instances, there are many more examples where it has been destructive. First, let's look at what ignites the anger fuse.

Typically, anger on the court is caused by a threat to one's ego. For example, it can occur when we make mistakes at critical times in a match or are losing—the most common factors that create negative emotion—because they make us think that we are failing. That is, our expectations are not being met in the moment (of course, there is always the possibility that the stress buildup off the court is a major contributor). This judgment and reaction to errors or "lost opportunities" create further tension and anxiety, which begins to hurt performance. However, we must be careful not to assume and label this type of reaction as negative unless our performance declines. Typically, when anger levels have reached a critical point, we may either begin overhitting, tanking, or making more mistakes, which, of course, only fuels the anger pump further. As our arousal levels rise, fluid strokes with proper biomechanics, effective strategy, and mental calmness become almost impossible to maintain.

Why then do we see some athletes actually performing at even higher levels when it is obvious that they are angry? To answer this question, let's observe the following scenario.

Jim is playing somebody he knows he can beat. But in this particular match he is down 4–3 in the first set and, from his perspective, playing rather poorly. At ad-out, after a long rally, he misses a relatively easy forehand (his strength) and goes down 5–3. Upon missing the forehand, Jim becomes incensed. He angrily screams to the heavens, "God, c'mon. Let's go!" But the scream has elements of extreme competitiveness in it. It has a different quality to it—not defeated or hopeless, but determined and competitive. Jim is absorbed in the match, pouring his heart out on every point and challenging himself. As you watch Jim play the next point after this outburst, you notice that he plays even more aggressively. You will not hear another outburst from Jim for quite a while, perhaps not until there is another important point he badly wants.

In the above scenario, Jim seems to be unaffected by his "passing" anger. Rather, the emotion is a reflection of his desire to play well and win, not of lasting disappointment and despair. In fact, Jim may even play better due to a rise in intensity, which makes him move his feet more quickly and helps him loosen up and go for his shots. If he can maintain this level of intensity and focus throughout the match without getting overly aroused for too long, he may play even better. The key is not to let your anger contaminate the next point.

However, in most instances, these emotional outbursts actually do contaminate your overall quality of play, affecting subsequent points and the match results. In the final analysis, it boils down to the quality of the anger, which is either fueled by challenge or by unrealistic expectations and despair. If it is the latter of the two, the problem is no longer a psychological one; it becomes a physical issue. When players become angry and negative, the body responds with a fight-or-flight response, sending a chemical known as cortisol to the brain, which creates muscle tension. And you know what muscle tension does to your strokes.

The ultimate question you have to ask yourself is whether your emotional reaction on the court, especially anger, hurts or helps your performance.

The best mentality on the court is to be so focused and absorbed in competition so you can have fun and go for your shots. Then anger becomes highly unlikely because of your involvement in the flow of your movements. As the pros often (though not always) demonstrate, errors are a natural part of any match. They don't become overly preoccupied with their winning passing shots—unless it is a critical point—nor do they blow up after missed opportunities. Their shots, points, and match results unfold over the course of the match, and they are keenly aware how their composure and reactions impact the momentum of every match. Andre Agassi, after the Australian Open in 2002, summed it up this way:

> There's a time to enjoy the good shots and a time to get upset about what happened, but it's not when you're out there. The question

you've got to ask yourself and answer is how do I make this the most difficult on my opponent, because he's struggling as much as you are. He's having to beat you, too, and the only way to do that is to think about the next point. It's quite a profound simplicity.

Agassi, in particular, became a master at literally turning his back after an error. He, like so many successful players, recognized how destructive anger can be during a match.

When you hit the court, take your high energy and competitiveness and channel it into every point. Keep the negative emotions off the court, and if you do reach a boiling point, try to turn this high energy into *more* competitiveness and pinpoint focus on the task at hand. When you get absorbed in the joy of hitting the ball, relishing the opportunity to challenge yourself, and keeping your ego caged in, you will no longer be a slave to your anger.

40

Trust Your Body

Human beings like to be in control. In tennis, the desire to control the outcome of the match or specific shots can cause anxiety and get in the way of executing your strokes on a certain level. You may worry about what will happen if you relax your body and trust your instinct. Trying to control your shots in this way makes you less willing to take the necessary risks or swing as freely as you would like through your shots. Letting go of control, trusting your shots, and accepting the outcome is imperative if you are going to ever play with true freedom on the court.

But, by now, you probably already know this, too. So what we really need to do is get at the heart of why you are controlling your shots so much and help you discover an alternative approach—one that helps you let go of control and trust your body. Here are some questions for you to consider first:

- When do you find yourself trying to control too much or trying too hard? Which strokes are you more inclined to do this with?

- What do you think would happen if you let go more and trusted your body without interference from your mind?

- Are there any benefits you receive from trying to control your strokes or the match in any way?

- What perspective would help you to let go and trust more?

- What old perspective would you be letting go of?

I really do understand how strange and difficult it is *not* to command yourself to hit certain shots when you have the opportunities. You want to play the right shot at the right time. I think what you really want is a guarantee that your choice will be met with success, don't you? So, in anticipation of hitting this shot, as your body prepares to perform what it's done in practice, it tightens up ever so slightly. You pull back just a hair, your head pops up as you peek at where you are hitting, and you don't fully finish the stroke. You look up to see the result as your opponent yells, "Out!" Your heart sinks. Did you make the wrong decision? How could you miss that? *That's it*, you say to yourself, *I'm not doing that again. I'm going to keep it in and wait for him to miss.* But wait. This mind-set is really only a guarantee that you will be relegated to playing safely and forcefully for the rest of your playing days.

Let's explore another approach. You've worked the point and have a backhand opening. You run to the ball with total clarity about where you will hit it next. Creating openings is your job as a player. You know this is only one shot and one point. You don't allow this one shot to determine whether you will win or lose. You trust your body to do what it has been trained to do in practice. You allow your upper body to stay loose as you maintain your intensity and conviction by not second-guessing yourself. Your brain and body know exactly what they are supposed to do, and you let them perform without interference.

To do this, begin to see a match from a larger perspective. Remember that a few isolated shots in all likelihood will not determine the outcome of the match. The only way you can actually play your best is by giving yourself the freedom to hit through your shots. You need to take the pressure off each individual shot and stop worrying about the outcome from point to point. Before you even go onto the court, set the goal that you will stay composed and trust your shots. Tell yourself you are willing to make errors if necessary but that you will trust your body to respond instinctively. Developing trust in your strokes and in your body, particularly when the score is close, is a gradual process, but it is worth it.

Let this be a goal and get familiar with the feeling when you successfully do it. Eventually, trusting your shots and keeping your mind out of the way will feel good, and you will begin doing it automatically more often. Remember, trust has to be unrelated to the outcome of your shot. The key is that you trust that this process will bring out your best tennis in the long run.

Become a Taskmaster
When Closing Out a Lead

Sitting slumped in her chair across from me, a young, nationally ranked junior tennis player told me about a recent match. "I can't believe what happened. I was serving for it, and I just froze up."

"What were you thinking?" I asked, as if I didn't know what was coming.

"I don't know. All of a sudden I thought, 'Wow, I'm up 5–3. What if I lose this? It would be awful.'"

She lost that match.

Fast-forward three months. This same player is playing in front of a dozen college coaches and goes up 5–3 in the third set. She approaches the line, as the possible win and importance of the match close in on her. She wipes it away and refocuses on executing her shots with authority.

She closes out her lead.

In the first example, as soon this player realized she was in a winning position, her mind skipped ahead to the finish line. She wanted to win and got caught up in the score and the meaning of the match. What she had been doing up until this moment—focusing on moving the ball around, attacking her returns and staying consistent—was out the window as her mind darted into the future and her body became overly aroused. Once she realized she still had a few games to win and she could actually lose, she became anxious that perhaps, after all this, she wouldn't be able to make it happen. At this point in her development as a young tennis player, she had no awareness of how to get her mind back on track, let alone realize that she even had a choice!

Many players in my sport psychology practice talk about their difficulty in closing out leads. Usually, the conversations focus on the anxiety and negative thoughts that creep in. More often than not, the prospect of winning or losing becomes the most disruptive internal distraction. And it's understandable. Most of us are achievement oriented. We like progress. We like winning. Winning is a great feeling, but when we're trying to close out a match and our minds jump to the finish line, to our triumphant handshake at the net, we get out of the moment. We deviate from executing our strategy and get overly attached to the score. This attachment makes us play a little tighter.

The reality is that our opponents, now facing the possibility of defeat, recognize that they must pick up their game. The errors we may have been appreciating from them just a few games before gradually diminish as their own anxiety morphs into a new mindset ("I better step it up or it's over"). But we're so close to being done and off the court, with a set in the bag, and only a couple more games to go, and we lose our focus just slightly, as our opponent wins a game or two. And then, of course, many of us think the momentum has shifted, which becomes a self-fulfilling prophecy.

The best thing you can do is to immediately *minimize* the importance of the score when you are in this situation. The fact that you are up a set and "almost there" is irrelevant as you prepare to serve at 5–3. Remember that your opponent will rarely just hand the match to you. There is no time to rest on your laurels or spend time thinking about the score. You need to get back to the next point and realize you have *a long way to go*. You must become a taskmaster and refocus on your strategy and play your game. Stay focused on the combination of shots that are working for you. Be careful not to get lulled into the downward spiral of negativity if your opponent's game picks up and you lose a few games. Do not panic. Stick to your guns and don't back down. The momentum is with you if you believe it is.

This approach will improve the odds of you turning those leads into victories. I know that shifting your focus like this, given the heat of the moment, is easier said than done, but it's a mind-set that will make a big difference. Remember, you are the one who controls where you put your attention at any moment. Nobody can take this away from you! Following this plan will likely turn your lead into a victory.

42

Quiet Your Mind

You probably already know that having a quiet mind will help you play better. The real issue is how can you effectively calm your mind given all the distractions you can experience at a tournament from the moment you arrive—players milling around the site and studying the draw sheet, uncertainty about when you will play, getting a proper warm-up, or getting locked into conversations you would rather not be having? If you don't have a way to manage all these potential distractions, your mind may run away on you.

Enter the deep breath. I know, you've heard about this technique more times than you can count. But do you really use it? And most importantly, are you really breathing properly? When I assess players' breathing patterns, even after they have practiced this technique for a few weeks, they often still breathe improperly. It's just too easy to fall back into old habits. Some players don't want to have to use a technique at all. They want to be able to have a quiet mind without having to work at it. So let this chapter be a reminder to nail this technique; you can then pull it out of the bag when you need it.

The truth is deep breathing is an amazingly powerful technique. When practiced regularly, it can lower your physical tension, help you refocus your attention, and take you out of your head in an instant. Believe it or not, learning to breathe properly and using this in competition will eventually win you matches you might otherwise have lost. Using your breath to quiet your mind has been used for thousands of years because it works.

This is more than just a technique. For many, it has become a way of life. It is the entry point to experiencing your "best self" in the present moment. The very act of focusing on your breathing brings your attention out of the head and into the body. The fact that we have the awareness and ability to manipulate our breathing allows us to alter our entire nervous system—something that, until recently, we've believed was largely out of our control.

How do you do this for maximum benefit? I've outlined the steps for you on the following pages. However, before you begin practicing this new skill, there are a few things you should know. If you don't practice this on a daily basis, it is likely that the impact of this technique and potential experience will be lost. This will feel mechanical at first, but eventually you will be able to use this technique anywhere you go, and it will help you. You need to see the results for yourself. If it helps you minimize your tendency to worry or throw your racquet, or calms your mind, you will be more likely to use it in matches.

Breathing properly requires you to first notice how you are breathing now. Most of us typically take shallow breaths from the chest when we are stressed or thinking negatively. It is an automatic fight-or-flight response that kicks in when we feel threatened in some way. Naturally, when we are faced with the prospects of making errors and losing or scoring our next big win, our autonomic nervous system is put to the test. To improve your breathing patterns, begin tracking how you are breathing throughout the day. Just notice from time to time if you are taking shallow breaths from your chest. Most likely you are. I'm still amazed how quickly this type of anxious breathing can set in. Once you catch yourself breathing like this, begin to experiment with deeper, diaphragmatic breaths. To train this, follow the guidelines below:

1. Place one hand on your abdomen and one hand on your chest.

2. Imagine that your stomach is a balloon you need to inflate.

3. Breathe in slowly to a count of four and exhale to a count of six.

4. Make sure your bottom hand is rising. If it is not rising, actually push your stomach out purposefully to get the feeling of breathing from your diaphragm as you breathe in.

5. Practice deep breathing five minutes per day for two weeks. By this time, your breaths should largely be coming from your stomach.

Additionally, to enhance your practice, once you become proficient and you are getting the majority of your breath from your stomach, take this skill to the next level. Practice the following steps to help make your breathing pattern even more effective.

1. As you exhale, focus your mind on your heart. In other words, allow your mind to drop down into your heart (this is your core energy source, where you are most powerful).

Pretend your mind is like an elevator that can literally drop down into your heart at will.

2. Notice how it feels to relax and let go. Letting go is the dominant feeling as you exhale.

3. Imagine that you are exhaling out all stress and tension. You may even want to visualize the color red as the stress and muscle tension pass through your lips as you exhale.

To use the breath on the court, take at least one or two deep breaths after each point to clear your head. Again, at first, it will feel very mechanical, but within a few weeks, it will feel more natural. Focusing on your breath as opposed to other thoughts that might creep in is far better anyway, even if it is mechanical at first. In fact, just the act of focusing on something else—beyond the score, judgment about your performance, or who's watching—will be helpful, even if you aren't doing the breathing exactly right just yet.

I was at the U.S. Open with a professional player a few years ago, and after he won his last round of qualifying and was in the main draw, the first thing he said to me was, "The breathing saved me."

Watch as this very simple skill helps you win and enjoy the game more than ever before.

43

Train Yourself to Be Loose

Most of us don't have a simple and effective way to decrease tension under pressure. We usually know it doesn't feel good when we're tense, but, of course, this doesn't change anything. We get tense and use too many muscles when we hit the ball. Though pre-shot routines, increasing the depth of your breathing, and playing aggressively regardless of your nerves can all help, sometimes players need to experience the true difference between tension and relaxation and train it to get the upper hand on their nerves.

With practice, you can learn to reduce muscle tension and lower your heart rate. Through years of reliable research studies, world-renowned doctor Herbert Benson, in his groundbreaking book *The Relaxation Response*, has proven that we are capable of learning how to relax ourselves deeply through awareness of our bodies and a systematic process known as *progressive muscle relaxation*. Progressive muscle relaxation, also known as PMR, has been widely received in hospitals worldwide as the single most effective technique to lower blood pressure and reduce stress. Its application in sports settings has also grown over the years and is a popular intervention used to reduce performance anxiety. Through Benson's research, it has been proven that people who practice this technique can significantly shift the way their bodies respond to stress in just six weeks. Instead of commanding yourself to relax or worrying about how you feel, you need to simply begin noticing where the tension is—most of the time the biggest culprits are shoulders and arms or legs.

I view this as another tool to help you access your optimal performance state on a consistent basis. The steps below will help guide you through progressive muscle relaxation.

1. Find a place where you will not be disturbed for at least ten to fifteen minutes.

2. Lie down on the floor or on a bed.

3. Begin by tensing your arms and hands, holding for seven seconds, and then relaxing for fifteen seconds. When you relax your muscles, continue taking deep breaths (in through your nose, out through your mouth) during the fifteen-second break as you observe the difference between the tension you felt and your relaxed muscles now. You will repeat this same process for the remaining body parts.

4. Tense your stomach (same time count as above). Repeat (optional).

5. Shrug your shoulders to your ears (same time count as above). Repeat (optional).

6. Bite down and tense your jaw (same time count as above). Repeat (optional).

7. Tense your entire face (same time count as above). Repeat (optional).

8. Tense your quads (same time count as above). Repeat (optional).

9. Tense your calves (same time count as above). Repeat (optional).

10. Tense your entire body (same time count as above). Repeat (optional).

As you see above, repeating each muscle group is optional. If you prefer the shorter version, you will not repeat each muscle group through this process.

In addition, you can also pair the feeling you have in your body with a word (for example, *loose, calm, let go,* etc.) as you exhale during the fifteen-second relaxation period to create a "cue" word you can use to help you recall this feeling when you feel overly tense or nervous.

To use this on the court, you will simply use the same technique of tensing and releasing your muscles on the changeovers as necessary. However, you will probably find the cue word most helpful between points to help you recall the feeling you have been training. Also, remember that simply practicing this exercise approximately four days per week will automatically improve your response to stress and reduce the activity of your autonomic nervous system. You should notice that your anxiety decreases within four to six weeks.

Some players don't like the idea of doing a technique like this because it makes them feel like there is something wrong with them. They believe that being loose should happen automatically. While some players do play looser than others under pressure for a variety of reasons, every player has figured out a way to access this performance state. Training your mind and body as you would your forehand or backhand only makes sense. Progressive muscle relaxation is one effective way to do this. Don't let your ego or insecurity get in the way of you finding a strategy that could make your body respond even better when that important situation arrives. You'll be glad you did when just one word relaxes your body just enough to rip that return down the line for the win.

44

Play With Controlled Aggression

Two years ago, I received a call from a coach working with a highly nationally ranked player, a talented player who could not seem to strike the balance between aggressive shots and taking some pace off at times. For her, anything less than completely whaling at the ball was impossible for her to accept. It was all or nothing. She was obviously winning quite a bit, but she struggled against any player who could handle her pace. She had only one gear. To make matters more difficult, if she wasn't playing perfectly—which is hard to do when you play in one gear—she would come unglued. Many young players I have worked with struggle with finding this balance. If you are having trouble mixing up your pace and playing smart, you need to consider improving your ability to play with "controlled aggression."

What does controlled aggression mean? It means you are hitting the ball aggressively, deep, and keeping your opponent pinned to the baseline, but it is not reckless. You know exactly what you are doing, there is a purpose behind your shots, and they are within your capability. You are not hitting shots you don't have and instead are choosing shots you know you own, and you are using them in the right situations. When you are playing with controlled aggression, you are typically on offense, sometimes simply holding your own, but not on defense. To improve your ability to play in this mode, focus on the depth of your shots and move your opponent around the court. Rather than trying to win the point in one or two shots, focus on "working the point" in an aggressive fashion. You are dictating play and are very clear about your strategy.

As I worked with the player I mention above, we discussed how she was thinking in black-and-white terms—an easy trap to fall into. We talked about her anxiety about *not* playing in her top gear and what this meant to her. As you might imagine, she prided herself on how well she could play when she went for every shot and how much she enjoyed the feedback and admiration from other people. To give this up initially was not terribly appealing. However, gradually, with some coaxing persistence from myself and the coach, coupled with a bit more awareness, she was able to add one more gear to her arsenal during our time. The coach worked on having her hit three different kinds of balls in practice so she could get more comfortable with a variety of paces and spins mixed in with her ripping winners. Eventually, she did improve her ability to play with more controlled aggression.

It is important for you to understand the benefit of playing in this way because otherwise you are not likely to embrace it. The truth is you will win matches if you can maintain a level of consistency with offense. Hitting the right shots at the right time and dictating play with an attitude of controlled aggression will help you avoid the extremes of overhitting or playing too conservatively.

45

Optimize Your Time
Between Points

Players are often surprised when they learn that in a two-set, ninety-minute singles match, they actually are striking the ball and in a rally for only approximately eighteen minutes. Recognizing that the remaining hour or more is spent walking from one side of the court to the other, picking up balls or resting on changeovers can be eye-opening for many players. With our mind's propensity to think, judge, and worry, the way we use this time can dramatically impact our performance. It is important to optimize our time between points.

While players' internal experiences between points can be very different, there are some fundamental guidelines for utilizing this precious time. If you are the kind of player who loses perspective in matches or becomes overly caught up in the score and outcome, or becomes self-conscious about your technique, it can help to use what I call a wide-angle lens when the point is finished. Give yourself permission to look up at the sky if you are playing outdoors, notice the trees, and let your mind slow down as you connect with something soothing and unrelated to the match. This will help you manage your energy more effectively and feel more refreshed for the next point. Five seconds should be plenty to give your mind a break (remember you have a total of twenty-five seconds to use if you need it).

Taking a deep breath as you notice your surroundings may enhance this feeling. Using the wide-angle lens periodically throughout the match will help you stay clearheaded and probably also raise your enjoyment of the match. Of course, you will always want to bring your attention back to the moment and next point after you take this pause.

On the other hand, some players are highly sensitive to their surroundings, and their "lens" is already as wide as it can go. They are focused on the people outside the court, their opponent's body language, and the players on the next court. If you find that this happens to you between points, you will benefit from using a specific object on which to focus your eyes—the ground, your racquet strings, or the ball in your or your opponent's hand. You could also use a spot on the back curtain or fence, which becomes your "home base" to remind yourself to narrow your attention to the task at hand. You'd be surprised how small techniques like this can go a long way in the heat of battle when your mind and eyes begin darting around.

It is also helpful to become aware of your current habits between points now. What do you tend to think about? In what situations are you inclined to rush?

I received a call from a frustrated parent telling me her daughter was distracted in matches and was constantly looking around between points. When I went to watch her play, I did notice that she was often taking her eyes off the court between points, mainly looking at the other matches being played next to her. She also seemed uptight during rallies. It turned out that she was feeling stressed and was actually glancing over at other matches because she was trying to take her mind off all the pressure. While this helped to lower her anxiety for a few moments between points, it wasn't helping her refocus on the next point very well. Once she realized that is was actually okay to recover between points and focus her attention on other things—besides a match that was also distracting—she learned to breathe and focus on her strings and her strategy. As she improved her ability to play with proper intensity and let the tension go between points, her game improved dramatically.

Jim Loehr, in his book, *The Power of Full Engagement*, describes the importance of balancing your energy.

> The science of periodization has become more precise and more sophisticated over the years, but the basic concept hasn't changed since it was first advanced nearly two thousand years ago. Following a period of activity, the body must replenish fundamental biochemical sources of energy ... Increase the intensity of the training or the performance demand, and it is necessary to commensurately increase the amount of energy renewal. Fail to do so and the athlete will experience a measurable deterioration in performance.

Don't waste the time you are given between points. Where you go in your head, whether on changeovers or approaching the line to serve or receive, will affect how your body feels. Working your way into your ideal mind-set has very much to do with how you manage your between-point time. Give your brain things to do that are productive and that will increase your energy so you can play the last game of the match like the first.

46

Set Performance Goals

Depending on your aspirations in the game and how often you plan to compete, setting performance goals can be extremely helpful. Many players talk about outcome goals they hope to achieve, such as being nationally or sectionally ranked, or becoming a professional tennis player, but they don't spend enough time setting goals that are more short-term and performance-based. Setting these goals based on your tournament schedule is critical because you want to make sure you are adequately prepared and rested leading up to your events.

Once you have an outcome goal, which can help motivate you, establish the aspects of your game that are most important to help you get there; these are called performance goals. To keep these goals short-term, plan in three-month intervals. Examples would be attacking the net ten times per set, improving your recovery time between points with a lower heart rate, increasing your first serve percentage to 60 percent, and increasing your depth on the backhand crosscourt. After you have recorded your performance goals, establish process goals—this will be the weekly and daily action items you need to put into your schedule. Using the examples above, these could be an approach-shot drill for thirty minutes twice per week, thirty minutes of interval cardio training four times per week within your target heart rate, twenty minutes of serves to both sides with targets after practice three times per week, and backhand crosscourt drills with cones three times per week for thirty minutes.

Your goals should reflect the time of year and your schedule. Ideally, you will have time before the heart of the season arrives to build up your cardio and strength for about four to six weeks, followed by strength training and, finally, simulated footwork exercises that mirror points on the court one to two weeks prior to the first tournament. Setting your goals based on your schedule will give you optimal stamina and help you manage your energy so you don't burn yourself out before the tournaments begin.

The key with goals is to make them flexible and realistic. Many players can get too ambitious and end up not following through. This can erode your confidence. It is better initially to make the goals small and achievable and gradually adjust them than to make them too lofty in the beginning.

Goals are helpful guardrails that can keep you on track on a daily basis. Once you establish what you want to achieve in a given year or over two to five years (the long-term or dream goals), you can begin to map out the necessary steps that will help you get there. The performance and process goals are the blueprints to your success and will keep you accountable. And, of course, we can all use some accountability, so you may want to find a confidant who will make sure you stay on track.

Choose Your Tennis Coach Wisely

"My coach doesn't really like to hear what I have to say," a client told me in a recent phone session. "He doesn't like a lot of input." Many players I work with talk about how confused they often feel with their games. "My coach tells me to hit the ball with the right technique, even if I miss. In the very next drill, he tells me to just do whatever it takes to finish the drill, even if I hit the ball wrong. I don't get it."

There are coaches who are experienced, thoughtful, and have a vision. And there are coaches who say a lot of the right things but have trouble applying it on a daily basis. You need to know the difference so you can choose your coach wisely.

How do you know if a coach is right for you? Before you commit to this relationship, meet with the coach and discuss his philosophy of coaching. Is he authoritative, collaborative, or a combination of the two? What does he emphasize in his coaching? How much does he integrate conditioning and mental training? After he shares his coaching style with you, notice what kinds of questions he asks you. How well does he listen and connect the dots related to you and your game? Is he personable and likeable? Chances are that the way he interacts with you in your first lesson will reflect at least part of his coaching style. Also, just because the prospective coach was a good player at one point doesn't mean he will be exceptional as a coach.

When a coach lectures too much and doesn't ask if what you are learning feels right or makes sense, this is a sign that you may be going down the wrong road. It takes a great deal of honest feedback and collaboration to weather the storms of skill development and winning and losing. A coach needs to take your thoughts, feelings, and personal idiosyncrasies into account. If he is not doing this and becomes dogmatic in his approach, be careful. Whether you like it or not, you have been sucked into *his* paradigm, and your needs and personal challenges may be swept aside. You become the casualty. You may find yourself stuck, the coach may get discouraged, tension builds, and the tug-of-war between you and the coach begins.

There is also a tendency for coaches to provide too much technical information at one time. This is not necessarily a reason to move on, by any means, but you will need to let your coach know that it is important for you to focus on a few adjustments at a time. I have seen too many players get lost in overanalysis because the coach is overly anxious about providing enough value (which means it is more about him or her and how they appear than your game). Often when this is happening, a coach may be focusing too much on symptoms and not on the cause. Be aware of this possibility so you can become more invested in your own development. Your feedback is critical, and if you are feeling overwhelmed or confused, there is probably a good reason for this.

Of course, there are many coaches who have a vision and can see how your game could look in the next few years. If your coach is experienced and has a good track record, you will want to trust his vision. However, if there is no give and take and little discussion about your thoughts along the way, you are going to want to speak up. If you don't, you are probably going to find yourself stagnating.

48

Never Give Up

You're down 5–2 in the third, and your mind is telling you to pack it in. It's a thought that is easy to believe, given the situation you are in. After all, you may not be playing that well, you've already tried everything you know, so what's the point? Well, you never know what might happen if you keep your head in the match. I am a big believer of never giving up until the match is over. Deep down, I think you are, too. Managing your mind is your greatest challenge because too often it will try to convince you to fold up your tent and go home.

It is likely that your mind will get overly consumed with the score when you are losing—a very natural place to focus when you're in a hole. However, this is where the secret lies. Because guess who is also focused on the score? That's right, your opponent. While your mind is telling you that the gap is too large to mount a comeback, you need to ignore it. The truth is, you may only need to grab a game or two before your opponent starts handing the rest over to you on a silver platter. This is where a "one point at a time" mentality will come in handy. Maybe even one shot at a time. But know this: Whatever you are feeling, I bet your opponent will feel the clamps twice as much after you win a game or two. Think about this statistic that came out of a study at Harvard: In a given match when you are playing an opponent of equal ability and can win just one point out of ten more than you did yesterday, the possibility of you winning rises from 50 to 90 percent!

One player shared with me the story of her comeback. She was in the state championships in high school, down 5–1 in the third set. Staring down the barrel of a 5–1 deficit, she knew her lifeline was pretty short. So, as she approached the deuce court to return serve, she suddenly stopped, turned, and walked back to the fence. Something deep within her spirit encouraged her to pull it together, give it all she had, and to fight until the end. This command—call it her deeper self, soul, whatever you want—was telling her to pull it together, to give it all she had, and to fight until the end. Point by point, rally by rally, she demonstrated that she wasn't going away easily. And, as is often the case, this created the "yips" for her opponent. Her opponent started going for too much (also common) and was making errors. Within about twenty minutes, she mounted a comeback and won the match 7–5 in the third set. She told me that, apparently, her opponent threw all her racquets in a nearby lake. I suppose losing a match like this after having such a lead was exactly what her opponent didn't want to do, and she pushed that fear button in her opponent by hanging in there.

To dig deeper, train yourself to take a few extra seconds to gather yourself when you are feeling negative or tense. Go back to the fence, look at your strings, and tell yourself to hang in there. Tell yourself that you can still win. You are still in it. Recall past matches when you prevailed from a deficit in a match. Think about how tense your opponent might feel with a lead. Then take a deep breath, pull up the fighting spirit within you, walk up to the line to serve or receive, and focus only on the next point. Mount your comeback one shot at a time.

You never know when the score may begin to tilt in your favor if you decide to fight until the end. Never give up.

49

Stop Mind Reading

The reason players worry about the opinions of others is because they are seeking validation. And tennis can be a brutal place to look for it. But whether you like it or not, it's important to realize that people don't spend half as much time thinking about your losses as you do.

I believe many players overemphasize both the status they achieve when they win and their fall from grace when they lose. Even if some elevated status is gained by winning, there is always a loss around the corner to put your ego in check. The truth is, win or lose, people are less caught up in your results than you think—unless you are in the top five in the world *and* extremely likeable. In this case, you are probably a role model and occupy a bit more bandwidth. However, outside of this select group, you might be surprised about how little time people spend wallowing in your losses or celebrating your wins.

What people want to see is good tennis. They want to see good rallies, heart, emotion, and clutch play. They want to lose themselves in the drama, and if they are involved in your development, they want to see signs of improvement. Those people who don't know you simply want to be inspired. They appreciate when you play superbly and win because it makes them feel that excellence is possible—or, of course, because it racks up a win for the team! Most people want to achieve a higher level themselves, and they appreciate you modeling that for them. People connect to the quality of a match, shots they observe, and the poise and confidence with which they are done. The result of a particular match or the status they may attribute to it, whether you won it or lost it, is usually transitory and, in the end, doesn't count nearly as much as *how* you do it.

Think about your experience when you watch a tennis match. Other than perhaps one of your favorite players in a big tournament, how upset do you get when someone you watch loses? How long do you spend thinking about the rise in that particular player's ranking? How long do you spend thinking about their amazing win or disappointing loss? My guess is that you get back to doing your own thing pretty quickly. This is simply human. We are involved in our own lives, yet we can also take joy in the drama of competition. They are not mutually exclusive. The point is to find a more balanced view of the meaning you may be attaching to your wins and losses and not beat yourself up so much.

A few years ago, I remember walking past a top player on the ATP Tour whom I knew on the practice court. He noticed that I was deep in thought after a session with a junior player and commented on my mood. "What's wrong?" he asked.

"Well, to be honest with you, I was just thinking about the pressure so many of these young players are putting on themselves. They worry so much about what other people are thinking of them."

Curious, he asked, "Well, what did you tell him?"

"I told him that after the match, the people he thought cared so much about his ranking and recent results were probably just thinking about what they were going to eat for lunch."

He responded, "Yeah. I know, it's probably true, but it's a tough habit to give up."

It is a hard concept for players to wrap their minds around—not worrying about letting other people down or blowing it in front of peers. So much of players' motivation can be based around other people's expectations and a desire to be validated. Letting go of this, or at least balancing it with a more rational view, can be disappointing because many players want to believe their results matter *that* much to others. The problem with this perspective is that it is this very need that gets in the way of players performing freely. Finding an inner drive that has more to do with your passion for the game and personal goals than other people's judgments is a far more peaceful and productive path to follow.

Next time your mind wanders off the court to the parents, fans, friends, and teammates, and you start thinking about other people's opinions of you, remind yourself that what everyone—including you—really wants is good competition and the excitement that is found in the game itself. And then get back to the joy of hitting through your shots and pouring your heart out as you run down the next ball.

50

Be Patient With the Process

We want results now. It is a challenge for most of us to be patient and allow ourselves time to develop and mature. This rush and belief that our time will run out unless we get "there" now is often counterproductive. It also doesn't give credence to the fact that you may be a late bloomer and have your best tennis still inside you. Andre Agassi proved this after his drop to number one hundred thirty-five in the world when he secured the number-one ranking two years later. Or Thomas Muster, unbelievably, after being hit by a car on the side of the highway and going through major physical therapy for over a year and a half, also rose to the number-one ranking in the world. What about Martina Navratilova, at the age of fifty, winning her tenth Grand Slam Mixed Doubles title in 2006? What about John McEnroe, at the age of forty-eight, winning a doubles title at the 2006 Siebel Open? What about forty-three-year-old Pancho Gonzáles beating nineteen-year-old Jimmy Connors? Then, what about Connors himself reaching the semifinals of the U.S. Open in a dramatic run at the age of thirty-nine?

When the pain of losing or a style of play eats away at you long enough, it becomes almost impossible *not* to change. Deep down, you know you can play better. You know you are capable of more. To tap this ability, commit to the process and be patient with yourself. Nothing happens overnight. Positive change takes time.

I made my own mistakes by rushing and forcing results and not building my game. Back in 1990, when I was playing the pro tour, I was impatient to gather ATP points. The late Tim Gullikson, a salt-of-the-earth guy and fantastic coach, told me during one of our practice sessions to take six months off from competing so he could revamp my game. While I had made enormous strides in just a few days with him, my impatience to improve my ranking and get on with it took hold of me. I didn't take him up on his offer. I believe my short-term view cost me considerable success at the time. This impatience can wreak havoc on our games in so many ways—forcing us to abandon a style of game in matches that would be best in the long run, spending too much time on parts of our games that won't yield maximum results, frustration with the win-loss record, and a lack of focus on developing our games.

Become aware of your patterns and be honest about your true mind-set. Enjoy the process of building your game. Take joy in your accomplishments and use your wins and losses as stepping stones. Hit the ball with renewed freedom as you allow the wins to simply emerge.

Afterword

It's Never Too Late to Play the Best Tennis of Your Life

Becoming more mentally tough is within your reach. It's also tempting to think that just by reading this book, it will happen on its own. It won't. Nothing worthwhile comes that easily. Improving your mental game, like technique, strategy, and physical conditioning, takes awareness, commitment, and execution. So I urge you to be patient with the process.

To apply the lessons in this book, I ask you to challenge old patterns. Become aware of what these patterns are—impatience, tentativeness, fear of losing, self-criticism, etc.—and commit to a new way of responding. Take one lesson per week from this book and focus on it. Make the lesson a performance goal in your next tournament. Remind yourself that you are playing for the long haul. Enjoy the process while you learn about yourself and your game. Take time and focus on what you are doing well and give yourself credit for the small improvements you are able to make.

Here's what happened to me: I became fed up with playing too conservatively. I knew I had more ability within me, and the thought of laying my racquet down one day knowing that I didn't approach the game in the right way was intolerable. At the same time, I developed a keen appreciation for the game and a sense of gratitude that I was alive and able to hit a yellow tennis ball. So I made a choice that I would change my behavior on the court—I would go for my shots, stay composed, get present, and learn to be loose, among other things. I held this above winning and losing. This was the hardest part, but it is where the rubber meets the road. The pain of playing the old way was greater than the score of the match. Once I committed to my new tennis "self," I began to play better and win more. I began to witness that my "new" tennis self was better. And there was no going back. The wins started piling up, and I wasn't even thinking about it the same way. The value of hitting the ball and carrying myself with confidence took precedence. And I started winning the mental game. You can do the same, and you will begin to play the best tennis of your life.

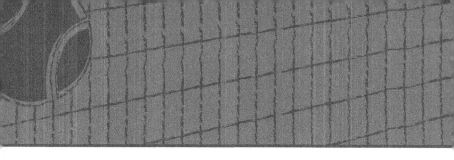

Suggested Readings

The following are some of my favorite resources that will add to the strategies I've described in this book.

Benson, Herbert. *The Relaxation Response.* New York: Morrow, 1975.

Csikszentmihalyi, Mihaly and Susan A. Jackson. *Flow in Sports.* Champaign, Illinois: Human Kinetics, 1999.

Csikszentmihalyi, Mihaly. *Finding Flow.* New York: Basic Books, 1997.

Gallwey, Tim. *The Inner Game of Tennis.* New York: Random House, 1974.

Garfield, Charles. *Peak Performance.* Los Angeles: J.P. Tarcher, 1984.

Gilbert, Brad. *Winning Ugly.* Secaucus, New Jersey: Carol Pub. Group, 1993.

Jeffers, Susan. *Feel the Fear and Do it Anyway.* San Diego: Harcourt, Brace, Jovanovich, 1987.

Kabat-Zinn, Jon. *Wherever You Go, There You Are.* New York: Hyperion, 1994.

Loehr, James. *Mental Toughness Training for Sports.* Lexington, Massachusetts: S. Greene Press, 1986.

Loehr, James. *The Power of Full Engagement.* New York, Free Press, 2003.

Millman, Dan. *The Way of the Peaceful Warrior.* Los Angeles: J.P. Tarcher, 1980.

Tolle, Eckhart. *The Power of Now.* Novato: New World Library, 1999.

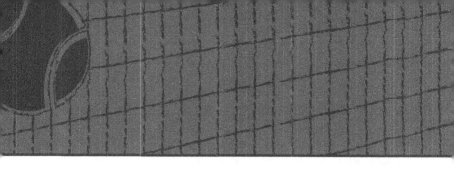

Index